Table Of Contents

An Overview

This anthology provides you with a wide selection of seasonal worship, drama, and children's resources from several popular authors. From Advent candle readings to Christmas plays, from children's stories and programs to inspirational readings, there's ample material to choose from. Whatever your congregation's size or worship style, you're sure to find something in *Christmas Treasures* that will make your Advent and Christmas services this year memorable ones. Copying privileges are included for all segments.

Litany For Advent And Christmas Candle Lighting (Elaine M. Ward) provides brief responsive prayers to be used when lighting the Advent candles during the four Sundays of Advent, Christmas Eve, and Epiphany. This resource features creative congregational activities in addition to moving prayers, and could be used for worship or as a Sunday school opener.

Christmas Treasures (R. H. Thompson) offers three different sets of short readings for Sundays in Advent and Christmas Eve. Perfect for the Advent candlelighting portion of the service, each two- to three-minute narrative links aspects of the nativity with events in our modern lives, both global and personal. While the readings capture the awe and wonder of Christ's birth, they also challenge worshipers to reflect on current issues and respond in ways that glorify the Lord. These pieces bring the entire church family together — the narratives can be easily read by any adult or teen, and each comes with a brief prayer written for younger children.

Six Christmas Testimonies (David H. Covington) is a set of dramatic readings depicting the Christmas events and their meaning from the viewpoint of six characters: John the Baptist, a magus, the innkeeper, Joseph, a shepherd, and Mary. Especially powerful when read in sequence as part of an Advent or Christmas Eve service, these concise readings are an excellent way to include members in the worship service.

The Christmas Gift (Janet K. Gardner) utilizes a creative approach that sets it apart from the typical Sunday school seasonal program. Based on Luke's Christmas scripture, this simple yet powerful play challenges worshipers to consider the question "What can I give him?" The answer, of course, is the gift of our talents — and the novel element of this presentation is the inclusion of a "talent show" within the play. Many of the speaking roles have only a few lines, and some parts can be combined for the small congregation. A prop list, set diagram, and sample rehearsal schedule are included to aid novice directors. With a performance time of fifteen minutes plus talent show time, this is a fun and exciting program that honors the integrity and wonder of Jesus' birth.

Two Christmas Dramas, "Who Are You In Bethlehem?" and "The Promise," (Rochelle M. Pennington) are dramatic presentations for children, adults, and the entire congregation that combine the reading of scripture and the singing of familiar hymns with brief narrations and dramatic roles that can be performed by any age. These inspirational services are flexible enough to be performed by as many participants as are available without requiring extensive memorization, making them great for congregations of any size. Each drama tells the Bethlehem story, yet focuses attention on how we respond to the Savior — asking if we have truly welcomed the babe into our hearts.

Four Christmas Plays (Mary Connealy) are flexible and Bible-based, with parts for young people of all ages. "Revelations Of Jesus" tells the story of Jesus' coming and how word of it spread, from the angel's visit to Mary, to the shepherds and the Wise Men, to a nation and then the world. "Given From Heaven/Received On Earth" takes a whimsical glimpse at the angels' preparations for the first Christmas, as they get the star ready, rehearse their song for the shepherds, and keep track of Mary and Joseph's search for lodging. "Nativity" is a simple, straightforward retelling of the nativity story. "If It Happened Today" is a somewhat longer presentation consisting of seven brief sketches connected by scripture readings and well-known songs. Each scene is a humorous but thought-provoking look at how we might react if some of the events in the Christmas story happened to us. A superb choice for a Sunday school holiday program, it has up to 33 speaking roles (including fourteen narrators) but is flexible enough to be done with fewer people. The skits are short enough to be easily memorized, and there are a variety of parts to suit different age levels. Performance time is approximately thirty minutes. Director's notes with suggestions for costumes, props, and staging are included.

Do You Hear What I Hear? (Cynthia E. Cowen) tells the story of Jesus' birth in song and narrative. Ideal for large or small Sunday school groups, it's an inspirational pageant with something for everyone, including songs for each grade level from kindergarten through fifth grade, dramatic scenes, and congregational hymns. This practical children's program provides an accessible yet compelling framework for your young people to experience the Christmas message.

Christmas Wonder (Elaine M. Ward) offers nine short children's sermons for Advent and Christmas in the form of imaginative stories. Each one uses the rich imagery of the season to illustrate God's grace and unconditional love, and includes brief talking points and a prayer. These are wonderful stories to share with children as you gather around the altar, that "manger" where stories are born and stored.

Reading The Christmas Eve Scriptures (Stan Purdum) is a simple but extremely effective scripture reading for two narrators. Interweaving several familiar Bible verses, the reading links the events of Christmas with those of Holy Week and Easter, providing a powerful flow of themes that underlines the larger story of the Incarnation. Though it's especially attractive for churches looking for meaningful worship presentations requiring a minimum of preparation, this reading will be a compelling part of any Christmas service.

Litany For Advent And Christmas Candle Lighting

For Sundays Of Advent, Christmas Eve, And Epiphany

Elaine M. Ward

Litany

First Sunday Of Advent

(*Light the first candle*)

Read Romans 13:11-12.

Leader: We light this candle to remind us of Paul's words to "put on the armor of light" which is the Lord Jesus Christ, and "wake from sleep."
   This is the time of year we light the candle of hope and love and light in order to put out the darkness of doubt.

All: Sing or read verse 6 of the hymn, "O Come, O Come, Emmanuel":
   O come, thou Dayspring, come and cheer
   our spirits by thy justice here;
   disperse the gloomy clouds of night,
   and death's dark shadows put to flight.
   Rejoice! Rejoice! Emmanuel shall come to thee, O Israel.

Leader: "Be strong, and let your heart take courage." (Psalm 27:14)

Prayer: (*Unison*) God of light and love, work through us to lighten the load of those who sit in darkness waiting for light. Amen.

Church Activity: Place the Nativity scene and Advent wreath on the altar at the worship center. The Wise Men should be placed at a distance from the creche and will come later. Display the words, "Put on the armor of light," above the altar.

Second Sunday Of Advent

(Light the first and then the second candle)

Read Romans 15:12-13.

Leader: We light this candle of joy and peace, believing in the God of hope by the power of the Holy Spirit.

All: What is that hope?

Leader: Paul wrote, "The root of Jesse shall come, the one who rises to rule the Gentiles; in him the Gentiles shall hope."

All: This is the season of hope.

Leader: So get ready!

All: This is our prayer.

Prayer: (*Unison*) Dear God, in you we hope. Open our hearts and minds to accept, know, and share that hope with others. Amen.

Church Activity: Sit in quiet and comfort and think about hope. Then on a sheet of paper list your blessings. Fold the paper and put it on the altar with thanksgiving and praise. Move the Wise Men a little closer to the manger.

Third Sunday Of Advent

(Light the first, second, and then the third candle)

Read James 5:7-10.

Leader: We light this candle of patience until the coming of the Lord, following the example of the prophets' suffering and patience.

All: We wait for the Lord.

Leader: While we wait, we celebrate the joy of the now. There is an old rabbinic saying that on Judgment Day we will have to give an account of every good thing we might have enjoyed and did not.

All: We wait for the Lord *with joy.*

Leader: James, the author of our Bible verse, wrote, "Whenever you face trials of any kind, count it all joy ..."

All: We wait for the Lord *with joy and patience.*

Leader: James also wrote, "Do not grumble against one another." This is the season to see the goodness in everyone and share the joy.

All: *With others* we wait for the Lord with patience and joy.

Prayer: *(Unison)* Dear God, let this be our prayer. Amen.

Church Activity: Write a letter to a grandparent, relative, or friend with whom you can share your love and joy.

Fourth Sunday Of Advent

(Light the first, second, third, and then the fourth candle)

Read Romans 1:1-7.

Leader: The time is coming nearer — the time to welcome Jesus Christ our Lord, descended from David and declared to be Son of God.

All: This is the one for whom we wait.

Leader: Are we ready to be obedient to his grace and peace and love?

All: Yes!

Leader: Then in Paul's words to the Romans, "Grace to you and peace from God our Father and the Lord Jesus Christ."

Prayer: *(Unison)* Dear God, we thank you for your extraordinary gift of love. Help us share it with others. Amen.

Church Activity: Look at the Nativity scene on the altar and move the Wise Men closer. Write the words, "Advent, Christmas, Epiphany," and any others you wish on paper and record what images come to mind. Write the words as fast as they come and then write other words triggered from what you have written.

Christmas Eve

(*Light the first, second, third, and fourth candle*)

Read Luke 2:1-20.

(*Light the white center candle as the "Christ candle"*)

Leader: "For God so loved the world, God gave his only son." (John 3:16)

All: That love came down at Christmas.

Leader:
> The gift of love begins in the heart,
> In the thought of the one who cares,
> In the time that it takes to think and plan
> For the love that the giver shares.
> The gift of love is a simple gift,
> No matter how large or how small,
> For the giver offering himself
> Is the greatest gift of all.

All: What can we give to God that is ours to give, in return for that love?

Leader: Saint Catherine of Siena was once asked this, and she replied that the only thing we can offer God that is of value to God is to give our love to people who are as unworthy of it as we are.

Prayer: (*Unison*)
> The world's at love and peace tonight.
> It started long ago,
> When one small baby in a stall
> Was born so all might know
> That God is never far away,
> Because of that first Christmas Day. Amen.

Church Activity: Create a Christmas cinquain, expressing in five lines your thoughts, feelings, and images about Christmas, using the following format:

1. The subject of the poem: Christmas
2. Two adjectives describing the subject: i.e., joyous, beautiful
3. Three verbs telling what the subject does: i.e., gives, receives, rejoices
4. A four-word phrase expressing your feeling about the subject: exhilarated by God's love
5. Another word for the subject: i.e., love

Bring the Wise Men a little closer to the manger.

Epiphany

Bring the Wise Men to the manger.

Read Matthew 2:1-12.

Leader: This is the day we celebrate the coming of the Wise Men from far away, bringing their gifts to Jesus.

All: Each person is invited to write a poem or prayer or draw a picture concerning the gift or gifts they would bring. We will place these things beside the manger.

Prayer: (*Unison*) Dear God, help us to share your great love and Good News with others. Amen.

Christmas Treasures

Advent And
Candle Lighting Readings
For Three Seasons

R. H. Thompson

Contents

Introduction

The purpose of the following readings for Advent candle lighting services is to capture a sense of the immense joy, wonder, and anticipation of Christmas. They are also meant to prompt thought and prayer about some of the wider issues in the world, linking with aspects of the Nativity, ultimately bringing praise and glory to our Lord, Jesus Christ!

The collection has worship material for three Advent/Christmas seasons. The series for each of the three years follows the same format: five narratives with prayers, and optional places for lighting the Advent candles. Scripture references are included with some. Each group of readings has been written to include all ages in the church family: the narratives are best suited to adult or teen readers, whereas the prayers have been written with children in mind. "Facing Jesus" (Series 2) is written as a three-part narrative and notes are included for the readers.

General suggestions
Readings:
- practice the piece aloud beforehand
- if possible, practice in the actual place where the narrative will be read, with a microphone (if appropriate)
- give special attention to speed, clarity, and expression
- make sure that any unfamiliar words and names are practiced

Each narrative takes from two to three minutes to read aloud. Some refer to global and current events, indicated by *. Although the facts were correct at time of writing, they will need to be updated. Websites such as World Vision and Jubilee USA provide details on these issues, and links to other sites that provide such information.

Lighting the Candles: Congregations enjoy watching this part of the service! The most natural time to light Advent candles is between a reading and prayer. It would likely be too distracting to do this during a reading — often times the match doesn't strike properly at first, or the candle lights but then flickers and dies and so has to be re-lit, or else the candle doesn't light at all!

Prayer: Each prayer provides both a time to reflect on the preceding reading and an opportunity to offer praise. The prayers have been written in simple language, specifically for elementary school-aged children to use, although they could be easily adjusted for adults. For many children, praying aloud in church may be a new experience, in which case, the above guidelines suggested for readers may apply.

Thank you! Thank you to all those involved in the worship ministries at the following churches, and their congregations, for so graciously testing the material:

Southside Community Church, Calgary, Alberta, Canada

Oundle Road Baptist Church, Peterborough, England

New Street Baptist Church, St. Neots, England

Bonavista Evangelical Missionary Church, Calgary, Alberta, Canada

Advent Candle Lighting
Series 1

Advent 1
Lights To The World

Some people put their Christmas lights up in November. Some people wait until the week before Christmas when there are no extra bulbs in the stores and you can't buy icicle lights anywhere. Some people just leave them up from one year to the next, and some people don't put any lights up at all.

Some houses have elaborate displays with floodlights and colored bulbs. Some houses have a simple row of lights running along the eaves. Some houses have figures of the Grinch or Santa and the reindeers or the Nativity. And some houses are decked out with lights everywhere: on every branch of every tree, twirled around bushes and shrubs, shaped into stars and snowflakes, and outlining every window and door. Those houses have Christmas music playing outside and usually get their picture in the newspaper.

Have you ever figured out why it is that when you put the lights away last year they were neat and tidy, but this year when you pulled them down from the top shelf with the other Christmas decorations, they were tangled and twisted into impossible knots? And when you finally straightened them out and plugged them in, they flickered half-heartedly and died? Or perhaps there was a bulb missing, so you decided that instead of searching the house for the spare bulbs that it was easier to go to the store and buy some more — but when you got there they had sold out because it's 4 o'clock on Christmas Eve. Now you've got a problem!

I wonder if that's how God thinks of us sometimes. As problems. We're supposed to shine for God. We're supposed to be lights to the world like a city on a hill. We're supposed to be good examples for others to follow. When God looks at us, listens to our secret thoughts, sees our selfish ways, our greedy hearts, our lack of compassion, and love for others, does he think that it would just be easier to toss us out with the trash — like we would throw out a string of burnt out, useless Christmas lights?

Thank goodness God doesn't do that. Thank goodness God loves us enough not to give up on us when we've given up on him. That God loves us enough to revive our indifferent spirits and renew our burnt out lives and mold those selfish, thoughtless, godless attitudes until we love God as we should. That God loves us enough to help us love others, and to shine like lights for him.

Don't be a burnt out Christmas bulb. Plug into God's power and shine for Jesus!

Light candle

Prayer: Lord Jesus, we thank you that you are the light of the world. We thank you for your great love. We ask that you will shine in our lives and through our lives, so that others may find you, too. Amen.

Advent 2
Greatly Troubled

Ah, Christmas shopping: the rustle of paper, the glitzy decorations, the angelic strains of carolers, hot apple cider, happy shoppers bidding each other cheerful Yuletide greetings, and of course, purchasing perfect gifts at perfect prices. Or was that a scene from a commercial?

Christmas carols have been playing in the mall since October. Frustrated shoppers are elbowing each other out of the way in the crush to buy the "Toy of the Year." And the most important phrase on everyone's lips seems to be, "Will the store exchange it if it's wrong?"

Mary was greatly troubled.

When we open the newspapers, switch on the television, log on to the Internet, bad news confronts us:
• Terrorism, wars, atrocities, refugees *
• Earthquakes, mudslides, volcano eruptions
• Third World poverty
• The AIDS epidemic

We can't change the world. Can anyone? Do you worry how events around the world will impact your life?

Mary was greatly troubled.

And what of our nation, the country we live in, the place we call home? There has been enough evidence in the past twelve months to prove our brokenness:
• Violence against children and by children *
• Plane crashes, car wrecks
• Floods, hurricanes, cyclones
• Political scandal, political unrest
• The economy
• Environmental issues

Sometimes we wonder whether life can get any more depressing than this!

Mary was greatly troubled.

What about our individual lives — our hopes and dreams, our fears, our job security, and long-term plans? Our complicated relationships and family situations? Health concerns and financial worries? Where does God fit into this?

Mary was greatly troubled.

Do the uncertainties of life trouble us? Perhaps not. Perhaps we don't think about them too much. Or perhaps they invade our minds in the stillness of night, or creep into our thoughts when we least expect them to.

In Luke's Gospel, chapter 1, we read that Mary was greatly troubled. An angel was standing before her. Mary was alone, just sweeping the floor, washing the dishes, thinking about what to prepare for supper maybe, when there he was. The angel had a message from the Lord God himself for her. Mary was greatly troubled by his words, "Greetings, you who are highly favored! The Lord is with you" (Luke 1:28).

Seeing her fear, the angel told her, "Do not be afraid. You have found favor with God" (Luke 1:30).

So Mary listened. She must have gotten over her fear, because she even questioned him, telling him, an angel, that what he was saying was impossible! By the time the angel left, Mary was no longer troubled. She trusted God and knew that he could do the impossible.

What troubles you? Do your troubles and concerns overwhelm you? Have you forgotten that with God all things are possible? In our world of uncertainties, be greatly troubled about the right thing — your relationship with the Almighty God — for it is God who holds our future.

Light candle

Prayer: Our Father, we praise you because you are Lord over every situation, every event, and every person in the world. When we are worried and afraid, help us to remember that you love us and are with us, always. We pray for people* all over the world who have suffered in the last year, and ask that your love and peace will fill their hearts. In Jesus' name. Amen.

(Service leaders may wish to insert specific current events, locally, nationally, and globally, from the past year that have had impact on our lives.)*

Advent 3
Christmas Treasures

Grandfather kept a small metal box in the attic. It was covered with a thick layer of dust. He had forgotten about it until times like these, when he had stumbled upon it in his annual search for the Christmas lights, but here it was, his treasure chest! He sat down and sighed, remembering the time when his own father had given it to him. Was it so long ago? Had so much time really passed by?

Clouds of dust rose into the air as his worn hands carefully opened the lid. He tenderly fingered each precious item. There was a hand-made fort with a chain drawbridge and painted metal soldiers, a well-worn copy of his favorite book, there were jigsaw puzzles — all had pieces missing no doubt — and a faded photograph of his parents, their picture yellowing around the curled up edges. And what was this? He turned it over in the palm of his hand, trying to remember. It looked like a piece of wood with numbers painted on one side. He couldn't recall exactly what it was, but he could remember when his father had given it to him. He had only been about five years old. It was during the war, and he had been ill in bed. His father had given him this piece of wood — a toy of some sort, he supposed — and an orange, which during the war was an expensive and rare treat. Grandfather felt tears sting his eyes. Old treasures. His treasures. They stirred up thoughts of those he had loved and of those who had loved him.

The shepherds had gone. It was just Mary, Joseph, and the baby Jesus in their crude shelter. Yet Mary treasured the things she had seen and heard, and pondered them in her heart. They were precious, wonderful words: an incredible tale of the night sky filled with angels praising God, announcing the birth of this baby — her baby — lying in the manger before her. She knew that it wasn't merely a story; it was true. She treasured these things. She thought about them. Over and over. Weighing everything up. Replaying the scenes in her head. Remembering everything. Wondering. Giving thanks to God.

What is it that we value most? Our homes and possessions; a healthy bank account? How about our golf handicap, our grades, or that promotion that we've worked so hard for? What about our friends, our health, or our image?

What does God treasure? What does God value most in us? Where does a pure heart and a godly life come on our priority list? Perhaps we should spend more time thinking about Jesus, reflecting on what he has done for us. Let's follow the example of the young Jewish girl, the new mom, the mother of Jesus.

"... Mary treasured all these things and pondered them in her heart" (Luke 2:19).

Light candle

Prayer: Lord Jesus, we love you! Help us as we worship you. Help us to think about your power and majesty, your mercy and humility, and your incredible love. Help us to honor you as we bring you our praise and worship. Amen.

Advent 4
With Us

A moment of glory: a gold medal at the Olympic Games, the winner of the Nobel Peace Prize, the newly-elected President, the champions of the Super Bowl. In the spotlight. Smiling for the camera. The center of attention and everyone loves them. It's their moment of glory.

Christmas reminds us that Jesus left the glory of heaven to live on earth like us. Heaven is where angels worship him. Where pain, hunger, jealousy, lies, insecurity, and danger do not exist. Heaven was his home. No character assassination, false accusations, or clever manipulation of the facts there. For a time he swapped the glory of heaven to live in the family of a Jewish carpenter. Why would Jesus leave heaven for this?

He lived on earth like us. He played with friends, grew out of clothes, ate food he didn't like, and experienced the growing pains of adolescence. He worked with his dad, encountered dissatisfied customers and customers who didn't pay their bill on time and customers who praised his workmanship. He got hungry and tired. He celebrated at weddings, discussed current events, cried at funerals, became angry with hypocrites, and taught people who didn't understand. He healed the sick. He socialized with drunks and prostitutes and lepers. He looked after his mother, went fishing, drew pictures, hiked around Galilee, and told stories. He confronted injustice and comforted the weary.

Immanuel means God with us. With all of us, all of the time. With us when life is great and when it isn't. With us whether we're starving in Africa, imprisoned in South America, exploited in China, dying in hospital, sunbathing in the Caribbean, trading stocks in New York City, talking politics in London, shopping at the mall, or trying to persuade a two-year old to eat zucchini. God is with us.

Think of another moment in time: cold nails, rough wood, sharp thorns. A dying man. Warm blood, life-blood, blood for life; my life and yours; God with us in life and with us in death. God with us in our final moments, in our last breath, in the very instant we die. And yet he did more than die — he conquered death. He went where we will never have to go, instead of us, to give us life that will last forever.

22

Jesus — taking us into glory, but not for a moment or a couple of weeks or even a lifetime; for eternity. Immanuel — God with us so that we can be with Him, and live in a glory that has no end.

Light candle

Prayer: Dear Lord Jesus, we are amazed at everything you have done for us, simply because you love us! This Christmas, remind us again of how deeply you love us and the price you paid so that we can receive your wonderful love and eternal life. Amen.

Christmas Eve
Finished!

It's all finished! Everything is ready. You never thought that this hour would arrive, but here it is. You can finally sit back and relax: the turkey is defrosted, the cookies are iced, the tree is trimmed, the relatives have arrived. And under the tree are nestled presents large and small, wrapped in shiny paper with ribbons and bows, just waiting to be unwrapped. Did you peek? When everyone else was out of the room, did you pick up that present with your name on it and peek? Just a little? Did you shake it, and turn it this way and that, just to guess what's inside? Come on, now, we won't tell. It's finished. It's all ready.

There was another similar cry of completion many years ago. But this cry echoed through the hills outside Jerusalem one bleak Friday. It was the desperate cry of a man dying on a cross. No! Listen more carefully. That's not defeat in his voice, that's not desperation. That's victory: "It is finished!" It's the cry of the triumphant Savior of the world (John 19:30).

It was done, over, completed, finished. The baby Jesus had become a man. He had made the blind see, the deaf hear, and cripples walk, run, and leap with joy. He had given new life to prostitutes, to cheaters, to outcasts of society. He had preached the Good News. He should have been a hero, yet men and women rejected him, laughed at him, then had him tortured, tried, and executed. And now it was over. His work was done. It was finished.

But don't leave Jesus on the cross. He didn't stay there. He didn't stay shrouded in tightly-wrapped grave clothes. He didn't stay in the tomb with its sealed entrance and Roman guards. He came back to life. Alive!

Jesus has done it all. It is finished. Everything is ready. He's knocking at the door of your heart. Stop awhile and listen. Do you hear it? Or are there louder voices clamoring for attention? The things that trouble and confuse you. Those things that you don't understand. The injustices in the world. The cruel twists that life throws at us. Put them aside just for a minute and listen. Just listen. He's still there, at the door of your heart. Shh, do you hear him now? "If anyone hears my voice and opens the door, I will go in and eat with him, and he with me" (Revelation 3:20).

Jesus is waiting for you to receive his gift. Forgiveness. Acceptance. Unconditional love. Eternal Life. How does that sound to the weary soul? He, the Almighty God, the Everlasting Father, the Prince of Peace, he is offering you the gift.

"For God so loved the world that he gave his one and only Son, that whoever believes in him shall not perish but have eternal life" (John 3:16).

It *is* finished! It's ready! The gift is here.

Will you take it?

Light candle

Prayer: Dear Lord and Loving Heavenly Father, you are the Mighty God and Prince of Peace! Thank you that because of your great mercy and forgiveness we can talk to you. We pray for people in our families and for our friends who don't know who you are and have never experienced your love or caught sight of your grace. And we pray that they will find you and accept your gift. In Jesus' name. Amen.

Advent Candle Lighting
Series 2

Advent 1
Numbers To Numb Us

It was an order. A Roman census. All persons in all countries under Roman rule must have their names listed in a register. They didn't have a choice. They had to go. Fathers, mothers, children, grandchildren, grandparents, babies: everyone. There was no option. No discussion. No exceptions or excuses. It didn't matter how convenient it was, what the weather was like, if you were sick, if you had no money, if it was your birthday, if you were getting married, if you were pregnant. It was a decree from Caesar Augustus and no one dared disobey. Statistics, it would seem, were as much a pain 2,000 years ago as they are today!

Numbers and statistics creep in everywhere — from the "Twelve Days of Christmas" to how many shopping days are left until Christmas! Numbers surround us. They fascinate us. Confuse us. Horrify us. Numbers tell us that in our world:
- over 1 billion people are living on less than one dollar a day, *
- the poorest countries owe the richest countries billions of dollars in debt,
- in the last year alone, about 30 million refugees, mostly women and children, were caught up in conflicts,
- more than 40 million people are living with AIDS, 95 percent of them in developing countries,
- globally a child dies from AIDS every minute.

Numbers like these overwhelm us. They are too big to understand, and we want to ignore them or explain them away; yet numbers such as these demand action. People have become statistics, and we don't see the individual impact — the emotions, the pain, and the hopes destroyed. Numbers can blind us, but these are people — people we call our brothers and sisters, who God loves just as dearly as he loves us.

There are 66 books in the Bible, twelve disciples, forty days in the wilderness, 33 years, and one cross. One cross that points the way towards no more disease, no more wars, no more tears, no more famine, no more orphans, no more debt, no more death. One God who became a baby. One God who died on the cross and rose from the grave simply because he loves us. Jesus — the One for all of us. The One who can put everything right.

There is no other statistic that compares.

Light candle

Prayer: Thank you, dear Lord, that every person in the world is precious to you. We don't know what to say when we see the horrible ways in which so many people are suffering, when we have so much. Thank you, Lord, that you are with them whatever they suffer. We ask that they will find comfort in you. And we ask forgiveness for the times when we don't see other people as our brothers and sisters. Open our eyes and change our hearts so that we will truly love each other. Amen.

(* In order to keep the figures current, they should be updated as per year. Figures compiled from World Vision, Jubilee Debt Campaign, and Global AIDS Alliance.)

Advent 2
Like The Shepherds

They had no idea what was about to happen. They could have been sitting around talking about the same old things: no money, the weather, politics, the job, no money. You can imagine them, a straggly group of shepherds, living in the fields, wishing that it were someone else who was working the night shift so that they could be at home sleeping. They were ordinary men doing an ordinary job. In fact, they were regarded by others in the community as being less than ordinary: simple, unintelligent, unimportant, insignificant.

Suddenly the hillside was bathed in light and filled with the voices of angels singing praises to God. You can imagine their fear and disbelief. You can imagine them rubbing their eyes against the glare. You can almost hear them saying, "Is this real?"

"Am I dreaming?"

God sent his angels to men with whom few people, if any, would want to be associated. And his glory shone around them. God chose this group of frightened shepherds to be the first people to hear that Jesus had been born. And even though the shepherds were obviously terrified, they listened to the message that the angels delivered.

"Do not be afraid! I bring you good news of great joy ... a Savior has been born to you; he is Christ the Lord" (Luke 2:10-11).

The shepherds heard what the angels said and recognized it was the Lord. They said to each other, "Let's go into Bethlehem and see this thing that has happened, which the Lord has told us about."

What was their conversation as they walked into Bethlehem? What went through their minds as they relived and recounted what they had seen? Did their families believe them? Did they, too, visit the baby Jesus? What impact did it have on their lives? Did they remember or make any connection, when, roughly thirty years later, a man claiming to be the Christ was crucified by the Romans?

What about us? Does God have a lasting impact on our lives? Do we, like the shepherds, tell those whom we love about Jesus? Maybe we're content just to listen to God. After all, we don't have hosts of angels bringing us news of incredible events, yet God wants us to do more than listen. He wants us to follow through on what he tells us, and, like the shepherds did, to "glorify and praise God for all the things they had seen."

The shepherds were ordinary people whom God loved. When they listened to what God said, they found Jesus. We, too, are ordinary people whom God loves. How do we react to the things God tells us through the Bible and other people? What impact does Jesus have on our lives each day? What impact do we let him have on the lives of others, through us?

Perhaps we all need to be more like the shepherds.

Light candle

Prayer: Dear Lord, our hearts are full of joy and thanks. We bring you glory and praise! Give us the faith to follow you whatever the circumstances. Work in our hearts and in our lives so that the people around us, our family and friends, will love you, too. Amen.

Advent 3
Christmas Leftovers

When Jesus was born, it was just an everyday event noticed by only his parents, a few shepherds, and an innkeeper who couldn't even find a room for Mary and Joseph at his inn. Jesus was just another statistic, another birth at a busy time in a busy town; another ordinary baby.

It's easy to forget that when Jesus was born, this was God himself in human form. Jesus came down to us because he loved us. There was no other way for us to be reconciled to God other than through the life and inevitable death of Jesus. God allowed himself to become human; to become a baby and before that, a fetus, an embryo — that vulnerable and helpless state that we so easily devalue today.

Even though we try to keep Jesus in the center of our festivities, sometimes it is still a crazy tangle of last minute shopping, running out of wrapping paper on Christmas Eve, remembering to mail cards, and a social whirl of carol concerts and dinners. Sometimes we get so caught up in Christmas preparations and traditions that we forget to prepare our hearts, and forget to teach our children and remind ourselves of what we are really celebrating.

Does it seem that sometimes at Christmas, we give God the contents of the trash can; the time that's left over? Those tired minutes at the end of the day? That frazzled prayer when the turkey dinner is ready but Grandpa and Grandma haven't arrived yet? Do we worship him in carols mumbled in familiarity while we mentally run through our "to-do" list? Is it as if we give God the trash, the scrunched up wrapping paper and empty boxes, instead of the real gift that was inside?

When the Wise Men followed the star, it led them to Jesus, the Mighty God in human form. We don't have to follow a star to find Jesus. Doesn't he deserve more than our Christmas leftovers?

Light candle

Prayer: Dear Lord, we worship you because you are God. We can't find enough words to tell you how much we love you, especially when we remember that you became a tiny baby — for us. Please forgive us when we allow holiday traditions to hide the real meaning of Christmas. Amen.

Advent 4
Bad News

The news took him by surprise. Life was going smoothly, just as planned, then it happened! Right out of the blue. Something so incredible that he couldn't even have dreamed it up. It threw him off balance. King Herod was troubled. Visitors with a strange story about following a star, a baby king, wanting to worship him. Herod called a meeting with his advisors. Imagine the furrowed brows, worried words, desperate hearts. A plan was concocted. It was nothing complicated or bizarre; in fact, it was very clever and sure to work. He met in secret with the Wise Men. He made a simple request, nothing that would arouse suspicion, "I'd like to visit the new king and give him my regards. Be sure to let me know where you find him."

Herod was unsettled and anxious. His whole future was at stake. And when his orders were not obeyed, when the Wise Men didn't return, his reaction was shocking. Keeping his future secure required drastic action. Find the baby! Kill him. Kill all the babies. In other words, mass murder.

You read your Bible. You read the newspaper. The two don't connect: "For unto us a child is born, unto us a son is given." *Two planes slam into the World Trade Center*. "And the government shall be upon his shoulder." *Thousands dead*. "And his name shall be called Wonderful Counselor." *Unrest continues in the Middle East*. "The Mighty God." *Refugees, squalid living conditions, oppression*. "The Everlasting Father." *Bombs fall. Unknown casualties*. "The Prince of Peace."

The news hits us every morning when we turn on the radio, when we read the newspaper, when we surf the Internet. One minute it's an ordinary morning, frying bacon, scrambling eggs, buttering toast; the next we're glued to our television watching and wondering, "What will happen next?" Our world is in disarray. We can't escape it. We can't avoid it. And we're troubled.

We search for answers. We ask questions. We try to make sense of it, but we can't. We shake our heads, weep, send money, and we do what we can. We pray but struggle for the words. Bad news troubles us and it's difficult to know the right reaction. How can we show compassion to the suffering or speak up for those who have no voice?

Whereas Herod was distracted by the news about Jesus, the news today can distract us from Jesus. The way that Herod saw it, the news about Jesus was bad news and he went to great trouble to find him. When bad news shakes us off balance, we should also look to Jesus — because whatever the world looks like, and however confusing it is, he still is the Mighty God, the Everlasting Father, the Prince of Peace.

Light candle

Prayer: Dear Lord and Father, help us to keep our eyes on you all the time, in good times and bad, because we know that you are Lord of all. Amen.

(* *Service leaders may wish to insert specific current events [locally, nationally, and globally] from the past year that have had impact on our lives.*)

Christmas Eve
Facing Jesus (3-part narrative)

Narrator 1: What do you say to someone who gives their baby an outrageous name?

Narrator 2: I don't know, but at least Mary and Joseph didn't have to worry about that, or wonder what color to paint the nursery — thanks to the angel.

Narrator 3: I don't think that there was a nursery in the stable, you know. In fact, it wasn't even a stable! Some people think it was a cave.

Narrator 1: Well, one thing's for sure: it wasn't the maternity unit at Bethlehem General.

Narrator 2: There were no clean sheets, no friendly nurses, no painkillers, and no hospital food — or maybe that's a good thing!

Narrator 3: The only "comforts" available to Mary were scratchy straw, a crude shelter, and simple shepherds visiting them.

Narrator 1: Even worse, no nurse to get rid of them when visiting time was over!

Narrator 2: Jesus wasn't even born in December! Scholars believe that the most likely time of year that Jesus was born was in October.

Narrator 1: So why do we make all the fuss? Why do we go to all the trouble of presents, decorations, Christmas traditions? It was only the birth of an insignificant Jewish baby, anyway.

Narrator 3: But the birth of any baby is special: a tiny, fragile, vulnerable, helpless, dependent, innocent being.

Narrator 2: So why is Jesus more special than all the other babies that are born?

Narrator 3: Because this baby was God himself! God came down to us in the form of a little baby.

Narrator 1: A baby with a destiny!

Narrator 2: He could have become a great political or religious leader,

Narrator 3: but his destiny was to die by crucifixion when he was only around thirty years of age. Jesus was willing to leave his heavenly throne, to live on earth, to be killed brutally, and to rise from the dead so that you, I, everyone, can be reconciled to God.

Narrator 1: Wait a minute! Aren't you talking about Easter?

Narrator 2: This a Christmas service! You know, the baby in the manger, the shepherds, the angels, the Wise Men, the star ...

Narrator 3: Okay, okay, but without Christmas, Easter could never have happened. Jesus, this tiny baby in the manger, was the Creator of the universe, but we only feel comfortable talking about him once or twice a year.

Narrator 1: Well, Santa Claus and Frosty the snowman *are* a lot less embarrassing!

Narrator 3: But Mary's baby is the same Jesus who hung on the cross, taking our punishment. This Jesus is the same person whom we blame, question, curse, ignore, disrespect, rebel against, and doubt.

Narrator 2: So what you're saying is that the baby Jesus is easy to look at, but facing Jesus hanging on the cross, with nails driven through his hands and a sword in his side, that is much more difficult.

Narrator 3: Mary was there at his birth. She went through the agonies of labor, and experienced the joy of gazing on the face of her newborn son. And thirty years later Mary was there at the cross, staring at the blood dripping down from his brow, watching his agony in death.

Narrator 2: I wonder if she saw the face of Almighty God or that of her first baby?

Narrator 3: One day we will all look at the face of Jesus; we will all bow down before him; we will all proclaim that he is Lord.

Narrator 2: We won't be looking at the face of the baby on a Christmas card or the man dying in agony on a cross,

Narrator 1: but the face of Jesus, the Almighty God, the King of all creation.

Narrator 3: *This* is whose birth we celebrate at Christmas.

Narrator 1: And if this Jesus is true ...

Narrator 2: ... then how can we walk away from him?

Narrator 3: This Christmas make the celebration complete; receive God's gift — Jesus!

(*Notes for narrators: the narrative should read like a conversation between three friends, with some sentences being completed by the next narrator. Practice reading the piece aloud several times in order to get a feel for its pace and spirit; some sentences are serious, others humorous. Avoid long pauses between sentences, and, if possible, to maintain smooth continuity of sentences, make sure that there are enough microphones for each narrator to have one's own.*)

Light candle

Prayer: Dear Father God, we want to thank you again for the great love that you have for each one of us. Thank you for your great compassion, for your mercy, for your forgiveness. We ask that your love will flood our hearts. We thank you for all the blessings you have given us, and most of all, we thank you for Jesus. Amen.

Advent Candle Lighting
Series 3

Advent 1
Christmas Trees

In the days before Christmas of 1990 people lined up for hours at the Hungarian border crossing into Romania. Christmas trees were tied roughly across cars, or carried on the shoulders of men and women who trudged across the border, anxious to celebrate Christmas with their friends and relatives.

For the previous forty years the country had been held in the iron grip of a cruel dictator. In the days leading up to Christmas just one year earlier the entire country had been in turmoil and on the brink of revolution. A pastor had been accused of preaching against the corrupt regime and as a consequence had been threatened with internal exile. His congregation had filled the street outside his home in protest. This uprising quickly turned into a revolt that spread across the country in a matter of days. When the army sided with the people, the revolution was over.

On Christmas Day the dictator and his wife were executed. Their reign of terror was over. The hope and anticipation that followed the revolution were likened to spring arriving early in Romania. Many people had been killed in the few days of bloodshed. In fighting for their country, ordinary citizens had given their lives to secure freedom for everyone else.

Christmas 1990 was the first free Christmas for many Romanians. They could meet freely with their friends and relatives. They could smile at strangers and exchange greetings with people in the street without fear of reprisals. They could celebrate the birth of Jesus openly, not wondering if they were being watched by the notorious secret police. The Christmas trees going into Romania can perhaps be seen as a symbol of their joy as they celebrated their new-found freedom.

What about us? How do we celebrate Christmas? Is it a genuine celebration of the wonder and awe of what happened in Bethlehem 2,000 years ago, or is it a time fraught with family tensions and financial worries? When the Romanians celebrated their first Christmas in freedom, it was a wonderful time, yet a time tinged with sadness as they remembered those who had died fighting against oppression.

At Christmastime we celebrate the birth of Jesus. We also remember his death, and that without it our lives would be bleak and empty. As we sit around our Christmas trees this year, let's remember to thank God for his love and the freedom that his blood has bought for us. Just as the Romanians celebrated the wonder of a free Christmas in 1990, let's celebrate the wonderful freedom that Jesus gives us every day.

Light candle

Prayer: Dear Lord Jesus, thank you for the freedom that you have given us and for the joy and peace that fill our hearts. Thank you, too, for the freedom we enjoy in our country. We pray for all people in the world who are suffering, and we ask that you will bring them comfort, peace, and the strength to go on. We also pray that you will speak to our hearts about what you want us to do when we see bad situations in the world. Amen.

Advent 2
Prepared?

It's a standing joke in our family. My sister never sends Christmas cards on time. They always arrive late. Once her Christmas cards arrived in May. No one could decide whether they were late from last year or early for next year! She freely admits that if Christmas were in March she still wouldn't be ready. It's the same with birthday cards, Mother's Day, Father's Day, Easter, and anniversaries. The card is always "in the mail." She's always late, but the cards always arrive. We aren't offended or upset or angry. We just know that she's never ready; she's not prepared.

Neither was the innkeeper. We don't know much about him; even his existence is assumed. Luke's Gospel doesn't mention an innkeeper specifically but someone had to tell the travelers that the inns were full. Perhaps it's not so much that the innkeeper wasn't prepared. He was prepared for the expected; he was ready for the huge crowds in town for the census. He had possibly even given up his own bed. His inn was probably packed to bursting. He probably knew that he'd have to turn people away. He just wasn't prepared for the unexpected. He didn't know that a king was about to be born. His inn was full. He had no more rooms. What could he do? He didn't know that this was Jesus knocking at the door.

None of us want to turn away the baby Jesus, but we're not quite so uncomfortable turning away from Jesus the man. We convince ourselves that our lives are full enough already; that it's not a big deal, religion. We'll wait until later, when we're older, when we've time to think it through properly and make an informed choice. We wait for an emergency, a crisis, a tragedy. Or we wait for a time when we're really going to need him.

On the other hand, perhaps we're not sure that we really want Jesus to love us as he wants to. We're afraid of giving everything and hold back on some area of our lives. Or else we're unsure of how much he loves us because sometimes he seems so far away, remote, not interested in us at all. So when Jesus knocks at the door, we're not prepared — like the Christmas cards arriving after the Easter eggs have been eaten, like the innkeeper who wasn't expecting the unexpected.

The grace of God will transform our thinking, it will change our attitudes; it will reach through us to others. God's love will bring us a peace that totally overwhelms us. Are we ready to let Jesus pour out his love and do the unexpected in our lives?

Light candle

Prayer: Lord Jesus, thank you that your love changes us! We can trust you with everything. Help us to give you every part of our lives, because we know that you love us. Amen.

Advent 3
Awestruck!

He was a respectable man with a secure job: a carpenter in a small town. He made things like chairs, tables, shelves, boxes, and crosses, perhaps. He was not yet married, but he would soon marry a local girl. It should have been perfect. Except that his young fiancée was pregnant. Listen carefully; can you hear the snickers? Do you see the people whispering behind their hands? "He's a fool to marry her!"

"He doesn't deserve someone like *that*!"

Did you listen to the rumor? "Well, *whose* baby is it, anyway?" — that one would keep people talking for months, years, centuries.

But the carpenter had seen an angel; he knew.

She was a teenager, engaged to be married. Her girlhood dreams were about to come true. But there was a snag: she was pregnant. The baby she was carrying did not belong to the man she was supposed to marry. Can you feel the shame, the embarrassment? Do you hear the gossips? "I always thought that she was such a good girl."

"What a pity."

"What a shame."

"What a waste of her life."

"How could she be so careless?"

But the girl had seen an angel; she knew.

Joseph and Mary knew that this was no ordinary baby. Oh, they didn't properly understand. Could you? They knew that this baby was the Almighty God. An angel had told them. This tiny being growing inside her, kicking at her ribs, giving her heartburn, changing her youthful figure — this was God himself. They knew.

After the baby had been born, they took him to the Temple in Jerusalem, and presented him to the Lord. As they stood in the temple court, they were amazed at the words of Simeon and Anna, two people who loved God and who praised him for the baby. Salvation. Promise. Blessed. Destiny. Sign. Redemption. Mary and Joseph marveled at these words.

How's that carpenter now? Not such a fool. And that teenage girl? Not so careless. They had seen an angel. They had listened to the message from God and believed it. They had cradled Jesus in their arms, heard his tiny cry, kissed his newborn brow, felt the grip of his fingers clutching theirs. They had felt the warmth of his body snuggle against them, heard his contented gurgle, and gazed into his eyes; they knew.

Do we marvel, too? Perhaps the Christmas story has become ordinary and familiar. After all, we hear it every year; it's nothing new. Or are we surprised by tears of joy, wonder, and amazement when we read about the incredible gift that God has given us in Jesus?

Be in awe of him. Step back and stand in the temple courts with Mary and Joseph, and marvel at what was said about Jesus.

Light candle

Prayer: Lord, you are awesome! We are amazed by your deep love for every single human being. We marvel that you, Holy God, became a baby. And that you, the Creator of everything, became dependent on earthly parents. Our hearts are overflowing with thanks, and we praise you, Lord! Amen.

Advent 4
Refugees

Huddled under a flimsy tent that offers scant protection from the cold wind and rain, they sit, hunched together, waiting for the next shells to shatter the air, and for the next bullets to cut across the sky. With bare feet splashing in the mud, children play near their hideout in the forest, while their parents collect wood and wonder if it's safe to return to their bombed-out houses. Peering through crude barbed-wire fences like caged animals at the zoo, wide and worried eyes stare out, wondering if freedom will ever be theirs. Her face slashed for a piece of bread, a woman cradles her baby in her arms, and wonders what happened to humanity.

Driven from their homes by natural disasters, civil wars, and poverty, refugees are everywhere. Just to live in freedom comes at a high price for them, sometimes costing their lives. For some it will never come at all. Driven from their own countries, from all that is familiar, they have fled the atrocities that haunt their memories. They find themselves in lands where the language is different, the food is different, and the customs are different, and where they don't have the same rights; they are refugees.

God's plan to save the human race from disaster involved sending his own son, Jesus, to earth in the form of a baby. Fleeing for their lives, Mary and Joseph escaped at dead of night into Egypt, a foreign country not exactly on the best terms with their own. They left behind their families, friends, a home, a job, and all with no knowledge of when they would return. Jesus, the preschool child to whom the Wise Men had brought gifts, had become a refugee.

As we prepare for Christmas in our homes, with our families, in the relative safety of North America, let's remember those who often, through no fault of their own, do not have this luxury. Let us remember people who in the past year have lost their homes and possessions, and have seen those whom they love killed by stray bullets or land mines or deliberately massacred. They are ordinary people, like us, but they have been displaced and have nothing, and now have the added stigma of being refugees. Although we cannot understand the tragedy that life has handed them, we know that Jesus does understand because he lived it; he is with them. He understands their plight, their desperation, their rejection, and their grief. He is Wonderful. He is Counselor. May he also be the Prince of Peace in the lives of us all.

Light candle

Prayer: Our Lord and Loving Father, we want to pray for people who are refugees all over the world *. Please give us compassion, love, and deep concern for them and their futures. Please forgive us when we ignore their situations and don't understand how difficult it is for them just to stay alive. Be with them, we pray. In Jesus' name. Amen.

(If desired, provide actual examples of locations of current refugees, such as, across Africa, Asia, and so on.)*

Christmas Eve
The Greatest Gift

"You never say, 'Yes!' " The child pouts and stomps across the room.

"You can't ride your scooter on the road. It's dangerous!" the mother replies. She's had this conversation a million times before.

The child persists. "I can't remember the last time you said, 'Yes!' "

"You're asking me the wrong questions," she says, and smiles. "Ask me if I love you. Ask me if I think you're incredibly awesome, if you're gorgeous, if you make me unbelievably happy. Ask me if I love you and if I'll always love you, no matter what, and I'll say, 'Yes!' "

When children receive a present at Christmas or on their birthdays or at any other time of the year, they rip into it to see what's inside. They try to pull the gifts out from the torn paper, and hurt their fingers trying to stretch the parcel tape or colored twine, and in the end get scissors to cut it open. They don't stop to appreciate the designer wrapping paper, color-coordinated ribbon and bows, or glittering gift tag. What they're interested in is what's inside; they just want the present! And without reminding, they're just as likely to forget to say, "Thank you!" They have no idea how much the gift cost. They don't think about the thought that went into selecting it. They just want to see what it is. It's as simple as this: they know it's for them — it has their name on it, they know who it's from, they know that person loves them, and they know it's going to be good.

Grace is God's gift to us. A gift for all humankind. A gift for us: for you, for me. Jesus describes the greatness of this love in the parable of the prodigal son. We catch a glimpse of this love that covers everything as the son returns home after spending all his money. Even as he goes home, his motives are mixed. He's got no money, his friends don't want to know him, he's been living rough, and he's hungry. But while he's still a long way off, not at the end of the street, or at the backyard gate, or knocking at the front door of the house, his father catches sight of him. He runs to meet him. He throws his arms around him. He can't stop kissing him, so happy he is to have his son home — and the son hasn't even said, "I'm sorry." When he tries to apologize, the father is talking about throwing a party in his honor and buying him new clothes. Forgiven! Accepted! Loved completely. Safe in the father's arms. Why would he want to be anywhere else?

And why would we? Open the gift. God's grace — it's the only thing we'll carry with us into eternity.

Light candle

Prayer: Lord Jesus, you are the King of kings, the Lord of all, the Prince of Peace, and our Creator, our Savior, our Friend, and our God. We are amazed that we can call you our God *and* our Friend. We worship and adore you! We are amazed by your deep love for us. We can never thank you enough. Amen.

Six Christmas Testimonies

Dramatic Readings

David H. Covington

Contents

Introduction

This series of dramatic readings for six speakers may be read in sequence as part of an Advent or Christmas Eve service. Costuming may be as simple or elaborate as desired.

As an alternative, the individual readings may be used as part of the worship services on the Sundays of Advent and on Christmas Eve.

Patterns for Christmas ornaments representing these characters of the Christmas story are included. Each week a new pattern may be distributed in the Sunday school classes for the children to make the ornaments. The ornaments may be hung on the Christmas tree in the sanctuary or the children may take them home. You might include making the ornaments as part of a congregational Advent event.

Enlarge each ornament pattern and make sufficient copies for your needs.

Ornament Patterns

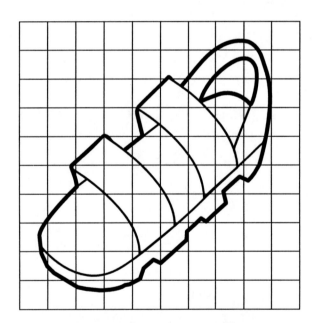

Sandal — John the Baptist

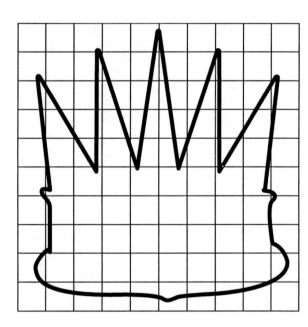

Crown — The Wise Man

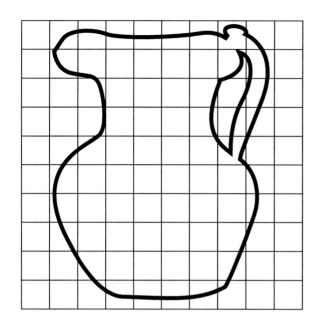

Pitcher — The Innkeeper

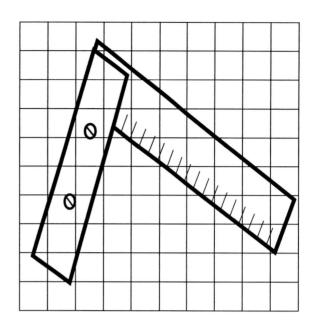

Carpenter's Square — Joseph

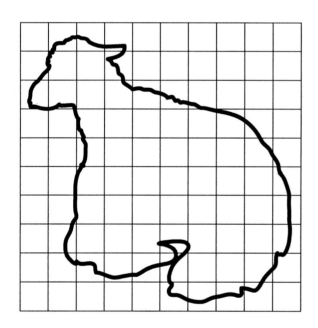

Sheep — Shepherd

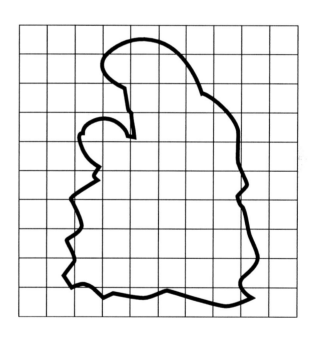

Mother and Child — Mary

Testimonies

John The Baptist

My name is John, an ordinary name.

I am *not* an ordinary man, however. I deny myself everything, that I might lack nothing.

I roam the desolate waste, living on sand and locusts. I lurch across the empty quarter, seeing caravans from afar. I walk unclothed in crooked circles among the lonely rocks, along the margins of existence.

I am ... reduced.

But I am not an aimless wanderer. I have been in this wilderness doing my job. It is important work. God's work.

I am preparing.

You must prepare as well. Do not wait. Begin. For something is about to happen, has already happened.

Listen. I have a message, a warning for you.

You must turn aside.

You are on the wrong path, the path to utter destruction. I have been in this heated inferno for a long time, but that is nothing compared ...

No, don't misunderstand. I am no voice of doom. I bring you hope!

Why, I wash people clean, make them pure. My followers arise anew, absolved.

I take no credit. I do not determine what is to come. I simply report the advent of a new time.

I have been wandering toward this river for years. I have arrived just in time, for in this place we will witness the beginning of God's world.

Of course you do not understand. These things I say are none too clear, even though the new age has already begun.

But believe this: Shortly, down that path will come the answer to all your questions. Deliverer, uplifter, restorer. Our lives will never be the same.

Magus

People seek me for advice. They call me wise, but I am not wise. I know little. But I do know this: I know that I do not know.

I have looked at dark skies for many years. I have seen the stars rise and fall in quiet arcs. Some say they tell the stories of our lives.

I do not believe this. The stars do not tell us of our fate. We see only our fears reflected there, and our hopes.

I spend my nights in solitude, in silence, looking from the corners of my eyes at small lights far off among the sleeping vastness.

These distant lights move but do not change. Time rolls and falls but nothing changes.

I hoped, once, to understand the universe, the scope of things, the meaning of life, the true significance. I no longer have these aspirations. Still I wait patiently, as if by habit, beyond hope, yet waiting.

But tonight ... tonight, I swear, I have seen — you may believe me — I have seen a — star. No. No mere star. A bright ... a shining ... an immense, expanding *illumination*! A light like no other. This was not subtle. I did not need to look askew to see it.

This star announces an arrival! I must go to greet this wonder. The silent stars have spoken to me after all. Something *has* happened; something has changed!

Innkeeper

Listen: I have something important I must tell you.

I'm not a religious man. I'm quite ordinary in every way. But —

Well, let me start at the beginning.

My name is — unimportant. Everyone calls me the same: Innkeeper. Keeper of spaces to sleep, temporary shelter from the dark and cold. I give travelers beds — for a price, and serve them food — for a price. A professional host. A seller of hospitality. I sell security by the night. I sell places to dream.

It's a modest inn. I work hard. I clean these rooms myself. I rent these rooms. I understand commerce. I am an honest man. I treat all the same, rich and poor. If they can pay, they stay. If they cannot, they go.

Times are good. This town is full — of human cattle coming in from the fields and villages seeking shelter and warmth, creeping through the streets at midnight, looking for a place to stay. Herod's census brings David's descendants here to Bethlehem, city of David, brings them home like sheep to be counted. And I count them too — as patrons. May there be no end to the counting!

Listen: I have a little stable, not much of a place, really. Just a few stalls for a donkey and a cow. Lots of dirty straw. The wind howls through, but it's good enough for livestock. It's around back, downwind of the inn.

And sometimes when the inn is crowded, like tonight, I put people in there, too. People with no other place to stay, people with — shall we say — limited means. And after all, a few extra coins couldn't hurt my income. An innkeeper with income — that has a good sound, doesn't it?

Tonight, I gave a space to the lost. A man and a woman — a girl, really, but heavy with child — so she could give birth under a roof.

And now I have heard such things! I do not understand. They have told me that this night — this night I have made room for — God. A small space. An humble place. But — room. Here in Bethlehem! In my inn!

I went to see for myself, and —

You will not credit this, but tonight — tonight, I — I have found God!

Joseph

This is hard for me. I am not a man of words. I am an ordinary man, a carpenter. My name is Joseph.

I'd rather speak with my hands, with a mallet and a chisel. I can read the grain of newly planed lumber. I can hammer pegs straight and true. I understand the softness of wood, and its firmness. I know how to fit corners, how to bevel edges, how to join strength to strength, how to bolster weakness.

I have a craft. I make useful things, beautiful things, and sell them. I work hard. I live in a village — you won't have heard of it: Nazareth, in Galilee.

And this — this is a strange business, strange from start to — to now, for I know it is not finished. It may never be finished. I don't understand what has happened.

I don't understand —

Look: I'm a righteous man. When I first heard about the baby, I was going to dismiss her, quietly, so as not to bring dishonor on her, but, surely you see, I couldn't continue with the marriage plans.

Then I had a dream. No one knows about this — you won't say anything, will you? I had a dream, an incredible dream.

This — this angel — came to me in the dream — I swear it — and told me not to be afraid. "Afraid of what?" I said. "Afraid of taking Mary as your wife," said the angel. "Why?" I said. "Because she is going to bear you a son that will also be your Father," said the angel. "Don't speak in riddles," I said. "The child is conceived of the Holy Spirit," he said. "You will call him Jesus, Savior, for he will save his people from their sins."

Now — this is the incredible part. I believed him. And I did what he commanded. I am taking Mary for my wife.

And this night — this night, I saw a wondrous thing! My world is not the same, cannot — ever — be the same. I saw a baby born. *My* son, my firstborn, and yet — my Father — my Lord, my hope, the living Word.

Shepherd

Hear me! Hear me! I have good news!

We were in the hills when —

What? Oh.

I'm a shepherd, an ordinary shepherd, not an educated man. I tend my flock, alone up in the hills except for my brothers. And the sheep, of course. We steer by stars at night when it's quiet.

Yes, that's right, we work hard. In the spring, we clip the wool and sell it. In the winter, we graze in the hills near the brook. We don't have much. We live on our feet. We move easily, unburdened by goods, unburdened by ills. We roam.

Nonetheless —

You must believe this, for it's true!

This night — this night, I have heard a frightening and wondrous thing!

My brothers and I were tending our flocks as usual. It was late, and dark, and quiet. We were dozing by the fire when — when the sky shone and an angel — yes, I know, but you must believe me — an angel appeared to us — you can ask my brothers, every word is true! And the angel — well, we were terrified if you want to know the truth, fell right down on the ground and didn't look up until the angel told us to — and the angel told us not to be afraid, but that's easier said, you know, and then the angel told us the Messiah was born in Bethlehem — in a stable, of all things!

Tonight, at least, I have knowledge that surpasses the wisdom of all humankind. I have heard the heavens speak and have seen the star sparkle, and I know that God is at work in the world. I have direction. I go to Bethlehem!

I have a Savior!

Mary

I don't know what to say. My name is Mary. I want you to know I'm no woman of the world. I'm an ordinary woman. I didn't ask to be here, didn't want to be in this place, this — stable. I didn't know it would be like this, far from my family, far from the comfort of my family's home.

I'm exhausted. I'm afraid for my child. It's dark in here, and dirty. The straw is rough and it smells. This is no place for a baby to be born. Especially not this child!

I did what I could. I wrapped him up in bands of cloth to keep him warm. I put him in some clean straw in the trough over there. But we need to go home. If only it weren't so far!

I am so tired, but I cannot sleep.

(*Pause*)

I have a secret.

An angel came to me, back when all this started. An angel. No, he just appeared when I was alone one day. And he told me ... No, he was — beautiful, and surrounded by light, and ... Of course I was afraid! But he told me not to be. And I felt calm, and I believed him. That's one of the ways I knew he was an angel. I felt so — peaceful.

And he told me I was blessed. Yes, "blessed among women," he said. I'm not exactly sure. But it sounded right, even though I didn't feel worthy. And he told me that I would have a son. That's right, a son. Who would be the savior of mankind. I know you don't believe me. I know I'm just a girl, and not a rich one at that. But I believed him. I didn't understand, but I believed. And I was at peace, even when I had to tell Joseph. That was a difficult time.

But not as difficult as this. This is the hardest thing I've ever done. I want to go home.

What? No, I still believe what the angel said. This night — this night, I did a wondrous thing. I birthed a child, a — child of God — a child from God. Through me! Life from my womb and — life for the world! My world — this world — is not the same, cannot — ever — be the same.

God kept His promise: I have a son!

The Christmas Gift

A Christmas Program
And Talent Show

Janet K. Gardner

Contents

Introduction

The Christmas Gift is a simple yet powerful play for all ages. With Luke's Christmas scripture as its backbone, the show challenges everyone with the question of Christian servitude. "What can I give you?" the Innkeeper asks baby Jesus. "All I have is this inn." Through the gifts and talents of the Orphans of Bethlehem, the possibilities are discussed and performed. Truly, no gift is too small for "We are his hands" and "We are his voice."

With a performance time of fifteen minutes plus talent show time *The Christmas Gift* is a simple, fun, and flexible show: comical skits, piano and musical performances, fun, old-fashioned "church" jokes. All give an exciting and hilarious flare to the wonder of the Christmas story.

Running Time
15 minutes plus talent show time

Large Speaking Parts
1. Innkeeper (28 lines)
2. Lead Orphan (14 lines — may perform in talent show)

Medium Speaking Parts
3. Narrator (10 lines — may be read from the podium)
4. Joseph (8 lines — may be same actor for the Traveler)
5. Traveler (4 lines — may be same actor for Joseph)
6. Mary (4 lines — may be same actor for the Traveler's Wife)
7. Little Orphan (4 lines — may perform in talent show)

1-Line Speaking Parts
8. Traveler's Wife (may be same actor for Mary)
9. Lead Angel
10. Artist Orphan (from Talent Show Performers)
11. Singing Orphan (from Talent Show Performers)

Talent Show Performers
The Orphans of Bethlehem
(Need at least 3 performers: musicians, artists, dancers, joke tellers, etc.)

Sunday School Choir
The Shepherds and Angels to sing two Christmas songs

Prop List

See "The Set Diagram" for suggested placement.

The Inn of Bethlehem backdrop
This can be a simply hung blanket or sheet painted or sewn with a door and window.

Signs
"Bethlehem," "Inn," "No Vacancy" (with "Vacancy" on back), and "Orphanage"
These signs can be easily printed in a large font on a computer and then mounted to cardboard. Attach wire loops to the cardboard for hanging. Use a wooden banner stand to hang the signs on hooks. Note that the "Orphanage" sign must be large enough to hang over both the "Inn" and "No Vacancy" signs so that at the end it reads "Bethlehem Orphanage."

Song Boards
These contain the words of the two Christmas songs that are sung by the performers. As with the Bethlehem signs, these Song Boards can also be printed on a computer and then mounted to cardboard. (Cardboard is recommended for all signs since it is stiffer and stands up better than normal poster board.) Also, it is recommended not to use song books since these can quickly become "toys" when placed into little hands.

Wooden Manger with a life-like doll as Baby Jesus

Two chairs for Mary and Joseph

Props for the Talent Show
Music stands, instruments, painting with paint brush, etc.

Stable Animals (*optional*)
These can be painted cardboard cut-outs or even stuffed animals placed around the manger area.

Sound system with Five Microphones (*optional, but strongly recommended*)
- Narrator's podium microphone
- Innkeeper microphone (wireless, if available)
- Two hand-held microphones for the performers — These are labeled with red and blue tape.
- Lead Angel's microphone — If available, use a second (portable) sound system behind the congregation since she will be proclaiming Jesus' birth from behind them.

The Christmas Songs

To help prevent any duplication of songs performed by the talented Orphans of Bethlehem, the two songs sung by the Shepherds and Angels after the talent show may be any Christmas song of the Director's choice. However, these songs should try to match their scenes as closely as possible. As such, the song "O Come, All Ye Faithful" is suggested for the arrival of the Shepherds and Angels into Bethlehem. For the closing finale, an upbeat Christmas celebration song like "Joy To The World" is recommended.

It is also suggested that the Director have the children sing these songs with some sort of a musical accompaniment: piano, prerecorded music cassette, and so on. *A cappella* can be very difficult and quite frustrating for young voices.

If there are only a couple shepherds and an angel making up the Sunday school children's choir, then it is recommended that the Orphans of Bethlehem join them in the singing of these songs.

The Talented Orphans Of Bethlehem

The Orphans provide the talent and much of the humor and fun to the show. Since not everyone can play the piano or a musical instrument, it is recommended that the performers of the talent show be sought out and cast first. Be very careful not to cast a young Beethoven as Joseph or in some other non-musical part. While the speaking roles are important — especially the Innkeeper's part — try not to miscast a talent. However, if someone insists on having both a speaking and talent show part, then the characters of the Lead Orphan and Little Orphan are available.

If there is a child who really wants to do something for the talent show but doesn't play an instrument, then the talents of artist and comedian are available. Skits work well, too, especially for older youth. For jokes, simple church humor works great and the joke, "Forrest Gump Goes To Heaven," has been included with this script as a resource idea.

Sample Joke: "Forrest Gump Goes To Heaven"

(Original author unknown)

Forrest Gump dies and goes to heaven. Before entering through the Pearly Gates, Saint Peter walks up to him and says, "Well, Forrest, it's certainly good to see you. However, heaven is filling up fast—so fast that we've had to start giving everyone an entrance exam."

Forrest responds: "It sure is good to see you, Saint Peter. I was lookin' forward to heaven, but nobody ever told me about a test. Sure hope it ain't too hard."

"Well," says Saint Peter, "it has only three questions:
1. What days of the week begin with the letter T?
2. How many seconds are there in a year?
3. What is God's first name?"

"Well," says Forrest, "let's see. The first one: 'How many days of the week begin with the letter T?' Shucks, that one's easy. Everybody knows that it'd be Today and Tomorrow."

The Saint's eyes widen. "Forrest!" he exclaims, "that's not what I was thinking, but you do have a point. I guess I didn't specify, so I'll give you credit for that answer. Now, how about the next question: How many seconds in a year?"

"Now that one's harder," says Forrest. "Hmm — let me think. Twelve. It's gotta be twelve."

Shocked, Saint Peter exclaims, "Twelve! Twelve! Forrest, how could you come up with twelve seconds in a year?"

"Aw, there's gotta be twelve: January second, February second, March second ..."

"Hold it," interrupts the Saint. "I see where you're going with this. It wasn't quite what I had in mind, but I'll give you credit for that one, too. Let's go to the last question: What is God's first name?"

"Hmm," thinks Forrest. "Oh, I know. It's Andy."

"Andy?" replies Saint Peter. "God's name is Andy?"

"Why, of course. You know, it's in that song we sing in church: 'Andy walks with me, Andy talks with me.' "

A Simple Rehearsal Schedule

(Yes — This really works!)

Important: Rehearsal time should *not* be substituted for Sunday school time. Just because a child attends Sunday school, it does not automatically mean that he or she will want to participate in the show. Remember, a key part to a successful Christmas show is having a cast that *wants* to be a part of it. As such, participation in the program should be strictly voluntary. If someone doesn't want to be a part of it, please don't force him. There's always next year.

Sunday school is, however, a great way to introduce the show's Christmas songs to the children, especially if your church doesn't have a formal children's choir. In this case, it's a matter of teaching them the songs and then asking who would be interested in singing them in the Christmas show. These volunteers become the shepherds and angels of the show.

To improve rehearsal attendance, it's recommended that all rehearsals (except for the dress rehearsal) be held immediately after the last church service. Have the performers bring a sack lunch if necessary. It's also recommended that all rehearsals be held in the same place where the actual show is to take place. This will greatly help the actors develop a solid feeling for where to stand, walk, etc. Likewise, rehearsing with two hand-held microphones (marked with red and blue tape) is also recommended. These microphones do not need to be working for these rehearsals, but are needed for the performers to get used to holding them.

Pre-Announcement Preparation

The Director should make arrangements to have the Christmas Show's casting call printed in the church bulletin and monthly newsletter.

8th Sunday before the Show

The First Announcement — The Director announces the show to the congregation, posts fliers about the casting call and need for talent show performers. Have scripts and a copy of the set diagram available for those interested in performing.

7th Sunday before the Show

The Second Announcement — The Director again announces the need for a cast: "Casting begins next Sunday immediately after church." Hand out scripts to all of those interested. Start making a list of interested performers and ask others for their participation.

6th Sunday before the Show

The Casting Call — Immediately after church, have the interested participants meet to select parts and to discuss talent performances. If more than one person is interested in the same part, have them audition for it.

5th Sunday before the Show

Rehearsal #1 — Characters 1 through 8: Narrator, Innkeeper, Traveler, Traveler's Wife, Lead Orphan, Little Orphan, Joseph, and Mary. (Note that the first few rehearsals are for the main cast only. The Talent show performers, who should be practicing at home, will be added on Rehearsals #4 and #5. Also at this time, the two Christmas songs sung by the Angels and Shepherds should start being taught to the Sunday school children's choir. Don't forget to use the Song Boards.)

Immediately after church, each rehearsal should last about one hour since it should be a complete run-through of the play from beginning to end, but will skip the talent show part which will be rehearsed later. If the rehearsal conflicts too much with lunch, then it may be necessary to ask the actors to bring a sack lunch.

4th Sunday before the Show

Rehearsal #2 — Characters 1 through 8. (If your church has a collection of Christmas costumes, they should be inventoried at this time. Do you have enough? The sewing talents of some supportive parents might be needed here.)

3rd Sunday before the Show

Rehearsal #3 — Characters 1 through 8.

2nd Sunday before the Show

Thanksgiving! — No rehearsal. (It's recommended not to have rehearsal over Thanksgiving weekend since this will probably conflict with family plans and create some frustration for the performers.)

1st Sunday before the Show

Rehearsal #4 — All cast, talent show performers, and Sunday school children's choir. (If your church has a collection of Christmas costumes, today is the day for them to be assigned to the performers. Do this after this rehearsal.)

The Day before the Show

Hours before the rehearsal, set up the stage, props, and microphones.

Rehearsal #5 — The Dress Rehearsal! This should be a mandatory rehearsal for everyone. Don't forget to have a sound technician available since the microphones will need to be working for this rehearsal. Also, consider having an evening rehearsal to improve attendance.

The Dress Rehearsal should have at least three complete run-throughs of the entire show. The final rehearsal should run without interruption by anyone — including the Director. When finished, all costumes should remain at the church so that one isn't accidentally left at home. Have an iron and safety pins ready. If something needs to be fixed, now is the time to do it. Remind the parents of those children who will be dressed in angel costumes to have their child wear white. A multi-colored *Star Wars* T-shirt looks a little tacky under an angel costume!

Show Time!

One hour before the show, all cast members should arrive to dress in their costumes. Although the parents might groan a little, the one-hour preparation time is critical to help plan coverage for any illnesses.

Sample Program Listing

**The Christmas Gift: A Christmas Program And Talent Show
by Janet K. Gardner**

Opening
    A dusty street in front of The Bethlehem Inn
    Narrator, Innkeeper, Traveler, and the Traveler's Wife
    (*See insert for Casting List*)

The Talented Orphans of Bethlehem
    (*List Talent Show acts here. For example ...*)
    "Forrest Gump Goes To Heaven"   (*performer's name*), Comedian

The Arrival of Mary and Joseph

The Arrival of the Shepherds and Angels
    "O Come, All Ye Faithful"   Sunday School Children's Choir

What Gift Are You?
    "Joy To The World"   All Cast and Congregation
    (*The Congregation is asked to join the cast in singing the third and fourth verses.*)

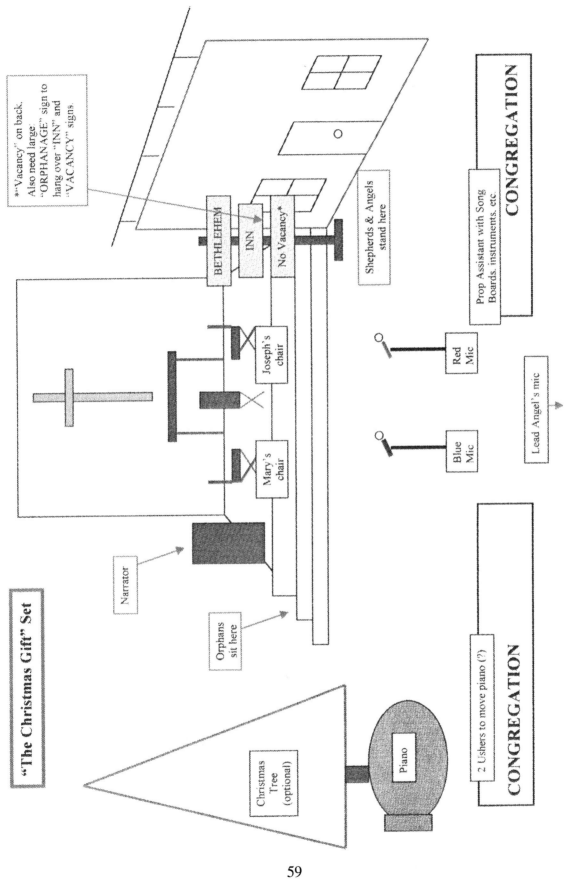

"The Christmas Gift" Set

*"Vacancy" on back. Also need large "ORPHANAGE" sign to hang over "INN" and "VACANCY" signs

BETHLEHEM

INN

No Vacancy*

Shepherds & Angels stand here

Joseph's chair

Mary's chair

Narrator

Orphans sit here

Christmas Tree (optional)

Piano

Prop Assistant with Song Boards, instruments, etc

CONGREGATION

Red Mic

Blue Mic

Lead Angel's mic

2 Ushers to move piano (?)

CONGREGATION

59

Script

Characters

Narrator — a formally dressed person with a deep, God-like voice

Innkeeper — a greedy, cranky person dressed in rich robes and jewelry; wears a lapel microphone throughout the program

Traveler — dressed in nice robes (may be same actor for Joseph)

Traveler's Wife — dressed in nice robes (may be same actor for Mary)

Lead Orphan — a tall, older youth with good stage presence and speaking voice

Little Orphan — simply dressed in a traditional biblical robe or cloak

Orphans of Bethlehem — the "Talent of Bethlehem" dressed in simple robes

Artist Orphan — one of the Orphans of Bethlehem

Singing Orphan — one of the Orphans of Bethlehem

Joseph, Father of Jesus — the strong-willed father-to-be

Mary, Mother of Jesus — the loving mother-to-be

Lead Angel — taller and older than the other angels

Shepherds — (these are the younger children from the Sunday school choir)

Angels — (these are the younger children from the Sunday school choir)

Setting

The dusty street in front of "The Bethlehem Inn." Next to the inn, there is a large sign reading "Vacancy" and a stable with a manger.

The Arrival Of The Travelers

(As the Congregation finishes singing a Christmas song, the Innkeeper walks up to the Inn's "Vacancy" sign and pretends to adjust it. Meanwhile, the Narrator steps up to the podium and opens the Bible. As he starts to read, the Innkeeper stops to listen.)

Narrator: *(On PODIUM microphone reads Luke 2:1-3)* "In those days, a decree went out from Caesar Augustus that all the world should be enrolled. This was the first enrollment, when Quirinius was governor of Syria. And all went to be enrolled, each to his own city —"

Innkeeper: *(To Narrator)* Whoa! Whoa! Wait a minute. You mean to tell me that *everyone* who's related to King David is coming here? To little Bethlehem! Are you crazy?

Narrator: Hey, I didn't write this stuff. I just read it, okay? But, what are you upset about? You're an innkeeper. Your rooms will be filled by tonight.

Innkeeper: Yeah! You know — you're right. Just think of all the money I'll make.

Narrator: Why, this town will be crawling with people. *(Enter the Traveler and his Wife, walking up the aisle and past the congregation)* In fact, here come some now. *(Narrator quietly sits down next to the podium)*

Traveler: *(Speaking off-microphone to his Wife, half-way up the aisle)* Hey, look — there's an inn. Let's go there.

Innkeeper: *(Greets Travelers)* Shalom, my friends.

Traveler: *(On RED microphone)* Shalom.

Innkeeper: Need a room? Only two left.

Traveler: Well, yes. One for us and one for my brother's family. But how much?

Innkeeper: 100 Denars — each!*

Traveler's Wife: *(On BLUE microphone)* So much? Why, that's four times the normal amount!

Innkeeper: Roman census, you know. Bethlehem is *not* that big, and there's a lot of people coming.

Traveler: Yeah. Yeah. I know. Fine, I'll take them. *(The Traveler pretends to pay the Innkeeper)* Come on. *(To wife)* Let's go find my brother.

(The Traveler and his Wife return the microphones to their stands and exit down the aisle as the Innkeeper goes over to the "Vacancy" sign and turns it over. It now reads "No Vacancy." As the Innkeeper fusses with the sign, the Orphans walk up the aisle.)

The Arrival Of The Orphans

Lead Orphan: *(To Orphans half-way up the aisle. Off-microphone)* Come on, everyone. This way. Hey, there's someone. Maybe he can help. *(On RED microphone)* Shalom, kind sir. My friends and I have no place to stay — and no food.

Little Orphan: *(Trying to be cute, and on the BLUE microphone)* And we are cold, too.

Lead Orphan: Please, sir, can you help?

Innkeeper: I have no more rooms, don't you see? *(Points to the sign)* No vacancy.

Lead Orphan: But, any place will do — even your stable over there. *(Points)*

Innkeeper: That old thing? You'd even stay there?

61

All Orphans: *(Nodding "Yes")* Uh — huh.

Innkeeper: Well, do you have any money?

Lead Orphan: Well, no, but we can work for you.

Innkeeper: But I already have servants. Now please go. I have nothing to give you — especially with the Romans taxing everything. Perhaps when the Messiah comes and delivers us from their hands, then I'll have some money to give you, but not now. Now go! Shoo. Find some other innkeeper to bother.

Little Orphan: But what if *he* were here now? What would you give *him*?

Innkeeper: Who? The other innkeeper? *(Timing pause for joke)*

Little Orphan: No, the *Messiah*. What would you give our Messiah?

Innkeeper: *(Laughing)* A room, of course — if he could pay for it. Now go. Shoo! *(Innkeeper resumes fussing with the No Vacancy Sign)*

Lead Orphan: *(To other orphans)* Come on, everyone. Let's find a giving heart elsewhere. *(Lead Orphan gives the RED microphone to Talent #1 for the next scene)*

(All Orphans meander over to the stable area which is center stage for the Talent Show, which now begins.)

The Talent Show

Little Orphan: *(On BLUE microphone)* Gee, the Messiah. Wouldn't it be great to see him? (Orphan Talent #1) What would you give him? *(Little Orphan gives BLUE microphone to Talent #2)*

Talent #1: *(On RED microphone)* Oh, I don't know. I suppose I'd (sing, dance, paint, play an instrument, and so on) for him.

(As Talent #1 begins to perform, the other Orphans sit down in their premarked places. During the show, the Innkeeper quietly stands off to the side, watching. When the talent is finished, everyone claps.)

Talent #1: Thank you. How about you, (Talent #2)? What would you do? What gift would you give our Lord?

(Talent #1 gives the RED microphone to Talent #3)

(The Talent Show continues with the above sequence of questions and answers repeating for each performer. For artists, the work is already completed and ready for display. The child pretends to complete the work there on stage with a brush, and so on, and then presents the finished piece, which is then displayed on an easel or music stand.)

(After everyone has performed, the BLUE microphone is returned to its stand while the Lead Orphan continues on the RED microphone.)

The Arrival Of Mary And Joseph

Lead Orphan: *(On RED microphone)* You know, *(standing up)* we all have gifts — even the Innkeeper. *(Pointing to him)*

Innkeeper: Yeah, right. Look, kids, I already told you: I have nothing to give you — or anyone else. *(Innkeeper grumbles, brushing them off, and walks behind the Inn's curtain, as if to enter)*

Lead Orphan: Well, what about you, Mr. Narrator? *(Meanders to RED mic's stand)*

Narrator: *(Startled)* What? Who me? *(Stands at the PODIUM)*

Lead Orphan: Yes, you. What gift would you give our Savior?

Narrator: Well — uh *(Startled by the question)* I'd — uh — probably just read to him. Would you like me to continue reading?

All Orphans: Yes. Tell us more.

(Lead Orphan quickly sets the RED microphone in its stand and sits with the group. Both microphones are now on their stands.)

Narrator: Let's see here. *(Looking for Luke 2:4-5)* "And everyone went to his own town to register." Oh, yes: "So Joseph also went up from the town of Nazareth in Galilee to Judea, to Bethlehem the town of David, because he belonged to the house and line of David."

(Enter Mary and Joseph walking up the center aisle.)

Narrator: "He went there to register with Mary, who was pledged to be married to him and was expecting a child."

Joseph: *(On RED microphone)* Look, Mary, another inn. Maybe this one will have a room.

Mary: *(On BLUE microphone)* Oh, Joseph, this one also says: "No Vacancy."

Joseph: Well, let's ask anyway. God will provide something for us. *(Knocks — or rings a hand bell)*

Innkeeper: *(Yelling from behind the Inn's curtain)* I told you street rats — No! *(Comes out)* Oh — I'm sorry. I thought you were someone else. Look, you're looking for a room right? *(Mary and Joseph nod "Yes")* Well, I'm sorry, everything is full — *(Laughs)* except for my stable over there. *(Pointing)*

Joseph: Okay.

Innkeeper: But, I was joking.

Joseph: I'm not.

Innkeeper: *(Surprised)* Well, okay. I charge 2 denari for each animal, so 6 denari — No, wait! *(Pointing to Mary's tummy)* You're pregnant. *8 denari!*

Mary: *(Disgusted)* Uhh! Joseph —

Joseph: It'll do, Mary. *(Pays Innkeeper)* It'll do.

(Mary and Joseph go up to the stable area and sit with the manger between them.)

Narrator: *(Reads)* "While they were there, the time came for the baby to be born, and she gave birth to her firstborn, a son —"

(Mary picks up baby Jesus, preplaced in the manger.)

Narrator: *(Continues reading)* "She wrapped him in cloths ... *(Slowly, as Mary then returns the baby to the manger)* and placed him in a manger, because there was no room for them in the inn."

Innkeeper: *(To Orphans)* Hey! You orphans there. I told you to leave. I have *paying* customers in that stable. Stop bothering them.

Joseph: *(Walks up to Innkeeper)* It's okay, really. We asked them to stay. They've been singing and dancing for us. *(Starts to walk the Innkeeper to his chair by the manger)*

Innkeeper: Oh, no. Look, I'm sorry that they've been bothering you.

Mary: But, they haven't. They're quite wonderful, really. We were just about to hear more of the story. Please join us.

Innkeeper: Me? Now? No, I need to get back to work.

Joseph: Sit down. Relax. The work can wait.

Innkeeper: *(Starts to sit down, but then pops back up)* No! I can't.

Joseph: *(Forcing the Innkeeper down into the chair)* Sit! Listen! *(Points to Narrator, cueing him to continue)*

The Arrival Of The Shepherds And Angels

Narrator: *(Reading Luke 2:8-13)* "And there were shepherds living out in the fields nearby, keeping watch over the flocks at night. An angel of the Lord appeared to them and the glory of the Lord shone around them, and they were terrified. But the angel said to them, 'Do not be afraid. I bring you good news of great joy that will be for all the people. Today in the town of David a Savior has been born to you; he is Christ the Lord. This will be a sign to you: You will find the babe wrapped in cloths and lying in a manger.'

"Suddenly a great company of the heavenly host appeared with the angel, praising God and saying:

Lead Angel: *(Appearing from behind the congregation and on a microphone. If possible, use a portable sound system's microphone so that the speakers are directly behind the congregation)* 'Glory to God in the highest, and on earth peace to all mankind on whom his favor rests!' "

(In awe, All Orphans, Mary holding the baby, and Joseph stand up.)

(Enter Angels and Shepherds singing "O Come, All Ye Faithful." They walk down the aisle and stand Stage Left, in front of the Inn in their premarked spots. Shepherds stand together and are closest to the Innkeeper. Orphans may sing with them. Prop Assistant displays Song Board.)

(Joseph gives RED microphone to Lead Orphan for next scene.)

(Mary gives BLUE microphone to Artist Orphan for next scene.)

What Can You Give Him? And Finale

(On the last verse, the Innkeeper walks over to the Shepherds, standing together.)

Innkeeper: Great! More orphans — orphaned *shepherds* at that!

Lead Orphan: *(On RED microphone, walks up to the Innkeeper)* But, we are all children of God. Children with gifts, with something to share.

Artist Orphan: *(On BLUE microphone)* Don't you see? We are his hands. *(Gives BLUE microphone to Singing Orphan)*

All: *(Raising their hands, except Innkeeper)* We are his hands. *(Clap!)*

Singing Orphan: *(On BLUE microphone)* We are his voice. *(Gives BLUE microphone to Mary)*

All: *(Except Innkeeper)* We are his voice.

Lead Orphan: What gift are you?

All: What gift are *you?* *(Pointing at the Innkeeper — and the congregation behind him — who is at the center of the stage area, ground level)*

Innkeeper: I don't know, okay? I don't know!

All: What can *you* give him? *(Again, pointing at Innkeeper — and congregation)*

Innkeeper: I-I'll give him — Oh, I don't know.

Lead Orphan: Go and look. *(Leading Innkeeper to the Babe)* Behold God's greatest gift — he who will die for our sins.

(Narrator prepares to hand the hidden "Orphanage" Sign to the Innkeeper.)

Innkeeper: *(Walks up to Mary holding the Babe so that he is evenly standing next to them and behind the manger. Slowly he says, as if singing)* What can I give you? What can I give? All I have is this Inn —

Mary: *(On BLUE microphone. Clearly and with a smile)* And love.

Innkeeper: That's it. What can I give him? I'll give him a room, of course!

Lead Orphan: *(Disgusted)* Oh, sure — "if he can *pay* for it," right?

Innkeeper: No. Not that kind of room. This kind — *(Suddenly reveals the large "Orphanage" sign)* An orphanage! I'll turn this inn into an orphanage!

(Everyone cheers and claps and then starts to sing Song #2: "Joy To The World." For added participation, have the congregation join in on the last two verses. Prop Assistant displays Song Board for Song #2. On the last verse, the entire cast forms a chorus line and as the song ends, they all raise their hands and then bow together.)

————————

Note: about $20 in US currency. 1 Denarius = 20 cents

Two Christmas Dramas

Who Are *You* In Bethlehem?

The Promise

Rochelle M. Pennington

Contents

Introduction

"Who Are *You* In Bethlehem?" is a complete Christmas program. Both children and adults participate with several speaking parts for young and old. There are on-stage roles for all the children, both speaking and non-speaking. The longer narration and scripture reading may be done by a number of older youth and adults. Hymn suggestions for the congregation are part of the program. Stage directions and simple costuming suggestions are included.

Speaking Parts
6 Narrators
3 Bible Readers
Donkey
3 Innkeepers
6 Small Stars
6 Angels
3 Shepherds
3 Wise Men

Non-speaking Parts
Lawn Boy
Kitchen Girl
Mary
Joseph
Large Star
Happy Child
Pastor

Who Are *You* In Bethlehem?

(Program And Script)

Congregational Hymn   "O Come, All Ye Faithful"

(During the last verse of the hymn above, Narrators 1 and 2 go to the left pulpit. Bible Reader 1 goes to the right pulpit.)

Narrator 1: Welcome! Together we have gathered here to remember and celebrate the greatest gift the world has ever received: the gift of God's Son, Jesus. Christmas after Christmas we rejoice in watching nativity plays which take us back to the blessed happenings in Bethlehem. Tonight we will return once again to Bethlehem, but this time we will go there unlike ever before: we are going to search not only for the Christ Child, but *for ourselves* as well *(Pauses)* for we are *all* there. In the words of our opening hymn *(Pauses and says the next words slowly and with rhythmic emphasis)* "O come ye, O come ye, to Bethlehem."

Narrator 2: We will meet the seldom-regarded and often-overlooked donkey first.

(Donkey enters.)

Donkey: My owner, Joseph, received word that the Roman government had issued a tax order. Everyone was required to go to the city from where their ancestors had come and sign up. This meant that Joseph needed to leave Nazareth where he was living and travel to Bethlehem. What a difficult time for this news to come! You see, Joseph's wife Mary was about to give birth to the Son of God at any moment! I couldn't see Mary making the seventy-mile trip on foot through all those dangerous hills, so I carried her. Although the hills were steep and filled with thieves, God delivered us safely to the gates of Bethlehem.

(The Donkey remains at center stage and is joined by a boy dressed in bib overalls and carrying a rake, as well as an aproned girl holding a pan she is wiping with a dish towel.)

Narrator 2: The donkey is not unlike so many Christians gathered right here who humbly serve in a quiet and simple way, often doing the strenuous jobs that are behind the scenes. Look closely. *(Pauses)* Is this *you*?

Reader 1: A reading from the Gospel of Matthew, chapter 23, verse 12: Jesus said, *"... and he that shall humble himself shall be exalted."*

(All the children join the Donkey, Lawn Boy, and Kitchen Girl at center stage for the next song.)

Children's Song   "The Friendly Beasts"

Narrator 1: Once inside the city of Bethlehem, the Holy Family came upon the innkeepers.

(Three Innkeepers enter.)

Innkeeper 1: I have no room for you! None at all! My inn is full!

Innkeeper 2: Go away! It is impossible for me to take you in!

Innkeeper 3: Okay, I guess I can make room, but you'll have to stay in the barn out back.

Reader 1: A reading from the book of Revelation, chapter 3, verse 20: Jesus said, *"Behold, I stand at the door and knock; if any man hear my voice, and open the door, I will come in to him...."*

Narrator 2: Jesus *still* stands at the door and knocks: *the door of our hearts.* Just like back in Bethlehem, how he hopes the door will open to welcome him in! Have you welcomed Jesus into your heart as an honored guest, or have you instead said, "Go away, I have no room for you"? Or maybe you have said to Jesus, "Come in to me, and I will make room for you," only to give him "the barn" of your heart, an area "out back" and usually forgotten. Look closely. *(Pauses)* Is this *you*?

Congregational Hymn   "O Little Town Of Bethlehem"

(During the first verse of the hymn above, Mary and Joseph enter front and are seated in the manger area. Mary cradles a doll. Mary and Joseph will stay in the manger area until the play concludes. During the last verse of the hymn, Narrators 1 and 2, along with Bible Reader 1, are seated. Once they are seated, Narrators 3 and 4 go to the left pulpit. Bible Reader 2 goes to the right pulpit.)

Reader 2: A reading from the Gospel of Luke, chapter 2, verses 6-7: *"And so it was, that, while they were there, the days were accomplished that she should be delivered. And she brought forth her firstborn son, and wrapped him in swaddling clothes, and laid him in a manger, because there was no room for them in the inn."*

Instrumental Piece   "Away In A Manger"

(The instrumental "Away In A Manger" piece can be a solo, duet, or trio performed by the children participating in the program who play a musical instrument. Any musical instruments are appropriate: flute, clarinet, violin, and so on.)

Narrator 3: Mary brought forth Jesus in a stable in Bethlehem. *Humbly* and *obediently* Mary had accepted God's will that she would be the mother of his son. When the angel Gabriel came to Mary to tell her that she had been chosen to give birth to God's Son, Mary responded, "Behold I am the handmaid of the Lord. Let it be to me according to thy word."

Narrator 4: Just like Mary, *each of us* is called by God to obey his will. His will ... *(holds up Bible)* ... is in his Word. Do *you* kneel in obedience and speak the words of Mary, "Let it be to me according to thy word"? Look closely. *(Pauses)* Is this *you*?

Reader 2: A reading from the Gospel of Matthew, chapter 2, verses 1-2: *"Now when Jesus was born in Bethlehem of Judea in the days of Herod the king, behold there came wise men from the east to Jerusalem, saying, 'Where is he that is born King of the Jews? For we have seen his star in the east, and are come to worship him.' "*

(Six small children dressed as Stars come forward and stand in a line. One older and taller child will stand behind them also dressed as a star. The costume of the Large Star should be extraordinary compared to the Small Stars.)

Small Stars: Sparkling, sparkling heavenly light, brightly shining in the night.

Narrator 3: Then came a star so gloriously bright, its flame engulfed the sky of night.

(The Large Star raises his hands and steps forward as the Small Stars part to make room for him. The Small Stars all gaze at the Large Star.)

Narrator 4: The star of Bethlehem appeared and shone with a brightness and radiance as never seen before. With *no words*, its *light* proclaimed the message of Jesus and brought travelers from distant lands. *(A child with a beaming smile comes up to stand in front of the Large Star and continues to smile and look completely joyous during the remaining narrations. Narrator 4 waits to continue reading the remaining two sentences which follow until the smiling child is in place.)* Just like the star of Bethlehem, there are Christians who allow the radiant light of Jesus within them to shine. *Really* shine! Without words, their testimony is their absolute joy and glow in the Lord. Look closely. *(Pauses)* Is this *you*?

Reader 2: A reading from the Gospel of John, chapter 8, verse 12, and also from the Gospel of Luke, chapter 11, verses 33-36: Jesus said, *"I am the light of the world: he that followeth me shall not walk in darkness, but shall have the Light of Life." "No man, when he hath lighted a candle, putteth it in a secret place, neither under a bushel, but on a candlestick, that they which come in may see the light."*

(All the children join the Stars and the Happy Child at center stage for the next song.)

Children's Song   "This Little Light Of Mine"

(After the song, all the children sit down, including Narrators 3, 4, and Bible Reader 2. Narrators 5 and 6 go to the left pulpit. Bible Reader 3 goes to the right pulpit. Shepherds and Angels gather at center front.)

Reader 3: A reading from the Gospel of Luke, chapter 2, verses 8-13: *And there were in the same country shepherds abiding in the field, keeping watch over their flock by night. And, lo, the angel of the Lord came upon them, and the glory of the Lord shone round about them: and they were sore afraid. And the angel said unto them:*

Angel 1: Fear not: for, behold, I bring you good tidings of great joy, which shall be to all people. For unto you is born this day in the city of David a Savior, which is Christ the Lord. And this shall be a sign unto you: Ye shall find the babe wrapped in swaddling clothes, lying in a manger.

Reader 3: *And suddenly there was with the angel a multitude of the heavenly host praising God.*

Angel 2: Glory! Glory! Glory!

Angel 3: Praise God!

Angel 4: Glory to God in the highest!

Angel 5: And on earth peace!

Angel 6: Good will to men!

All Angels: *("Fly" away from Shepherds exiting down the center and side aisles divided into three separate groups. While they are exiting, they will say the next words in unison.)* Glory! Glory! Glory! Glory to God in the highest!

Narrator 5: The angels of the Bethlehem story were filled with praise for God. "Glory! Glory! Glory! Glory to God in the highest!"

Narrator 6: Look closely. *(Pauses)* Is this *you*? *(A choir member comes forward now and sings a couple of lines of praise music)* Do *your* lips proclaim the praise of God? Do *your* words example those of the Psalmist? *"I will bless the Lord at all times. His praise shall continually be in my mouth."*

(Shepherds remain at center stage during the next hymn.)

Congregational Hymn   "Angels We Have Heard On High"

Reader 3: A reading from the Gospel of Luke, chapter 2, verses 15-18: *And it came to pass, as the angels were gone away from them into heaven, the shepherds said one to another:*

Shepherd 1: Let us now go even unto Bethlehem,

Shepherd 2: and see this thing which is come to pass,

Shepherd 3: which the Lord hath made known unto us.

(Shepherds turn and kneel at the manger scene.)

Reader 3: *And they came with haste, and found Mary and Joseph, and the babe lying in a manger. And when they had seen it, they made known abroad the saying which was told them concerning this child. And all they that heard it wondered at those things which were told them by the shepherds.*

(Shepherds stand and face the congregation.)

Shepherd 4: We have seen the Christ with our own eyes!

Shepherd 5: God's promised Messiah is come to Bethlehem!

Shepherd 6: The Savior of the world is come!

(Shepherds exit.)

Narrator 5: The shepherds were the first witnesses to Jesus. They took the message delivered unto them and "made it known *abroad.*" Look closely. *(Pauses)* Is this *you?*

(Church Pastor comes forward with his Bible and stands with the Shepherds.)

Narrator 6: The last words spoken by Jesus to his disciples were, "Go ye therefore, and teach all nations, baptizing them in the name of the Father, and of the Son, and of the Holy Ghost: teaching them to observe all things whatsoever I have commanded you. And, lo, I am with you always, even unto the end of the world." Has the message of Jesus been made known unto your heart? Have you, like the shepherds of Bethlehem, taken this message to others? In the words of Jesus: *Go ye therefore.*

(Wise Men enter and stand at center stage.)

Reader 3: A reading from the Gospel of Matthew, chapter 2, verses 1-2 and 9-11: *Now when Jesus was born in Bethlehem of Judea in the days of Herod the king, behold there came wise men from the east to Jerusalem, saying:*

Wise Man 1: Where is he that is born King of the Jews?

Wise Man 2: For we have seen his star in the east

Wise Man 3: and are come to worship him.

(During the Bible reading, the Wise Men will kneel at the manger area, present their gifts and then exit down the center aisle.)

Reader 3: *When they had heard the king, they departed; and, lo, the star which they saw in the east, went before them, till it came and stood over where the young child was. When they saw the star, they rejoiced with exceeding great joy. And when they were come into the house, they saw the young child with Mary his mother, and fell down, **and worshiped him**; and when they had opened their treasures, they presented unto him gifts: gold, frankincense, and myrrh.*

Narrator 5: *(With great emphasis)* "We have come to worship him."

Narrator 6: The Wise Men show the coming forth of adoration and worship. At *all costs* and *all struggles*, they were determined to kneel before the King of kings. For two years they journeyed from a far-off land. The Wise Men didn't say, "It's too much work to go and worship. We have no time to go and worship. We're much too busy and have other things to do." Look closely. *(Pauses)* Is this *you?*

Reader 3: A reading from the Gospel of Matthew, chapter 2, verses 13 and 16: *And when they were departed, behold, the angel of the Lord appeareth to Joseph in a dream, saying, "Arise, and take the young child and his mother, and flee into Egypt, and be thou there until I bring thee word: for Herod will seek the young child to destroy him." Then Herod, when he saw that he was mocked of the wise men, was exceedingly rageful, and sent forth, and slew all the children that were in Bethlehem, and in all the coasts thereof, from two years old and under, according to the time which he had diligently inquired of the wise men.*

Narrator 5: *Even the unbelievers* are found within the Bethlehem story in the person of Herod the king who wanted nothing more than the life and the name of Jesus silenced forever. But that didn't happen because "shepherds" of the message *kept coming* to tell "all that had been made known unto them abroad," and "donkeys" *kept coming* to serve in a humble and necessary way, and "angels" *kept coming* to strengthen the message with praise and adoration and glory unto the Lord, and "innkeepers" *kept coming* to fling the doors of their hearts wide open and welcome the Honored Guest in, and "Marys" *kept coming*, obedient to the will and the Word of God, and "wise men" *kept coming* to worship him and lay gifts before his throne, and "stars" *kept coming* to shine the message of infinite Light to the world.

Narrator 6: May this Christmas fill your heart with the gift of individual purpose which has been given unto you by God to glorify the message this his Son was born so long ago ... *in Bethlehem.*

Congregational Hymn   "Joy To The World"

Introduction

A complete Christmas program for the whole congregation, "The Promise" is presented in three scenes: The Prophecies, Bethlehem, and Shepherds And Angels. Speaking parts of various lengths allow all ages to participate, with the longer parts being assigned to older youth and adults. Congregational hymns and a carol sung by the children are included, as well as stage directions and simple costume suggestions.

Speaking Parts
4 Narrators
Micah
Isaiah
Bible Reader (as many as 8, if desired)
8 Angels
Mary
Joseph
Roman
3 Innkeepers
6 Shepherds
3 Wise Men

The Promise

(Program And Script)

Congregational Hymn   "O Come, All Ye Faithful"

Scene: The Prophecies

Narrator 1: Welcome! Together we have gathered here to remember and celebrate the greatest gift the world has ever received: the gift of God's son, Jesus. Although Jesus was born in a manger in Bethlehem 2,000 years ago, the story of Jesus began long before with the Old Testament prophets who spoke of his coming.

Narrator 2: A prophecy is a message from God that is brought forth to the people by a chosen prophet. Throughout the Old Testament of the Bible, as early as the first book of Genesis, God promised to send a Savior to deliver his people. These promises would come to pass according to God's Divine Plan. The birth of Jesus fulfilled *over 200* of these prophecies.

(Two Prophets enter front. The Prophet Micah is dressed in a simple robe. The Prophet Isaiah is dressed in a fine garment similar to the costumes of the Wise Men.)

Micah: Hear the word of God! My name is Micah and God has spoken to me. He has promised to send a Savior to the world. The Savior will come to the little town of Bethlehem.

Reader: A reading from the Old Testament book of the Prophet Micah, chapter 5, verse 2: *But thou, Bethlehem Ephratah, though thou be little among the thousands of Judah, yet out of thee shall he come forth unto me that is to be ruler in Israel; whose goings forth have been from old, from everlasting.*

Isaiah: My name is Isaiah and I have come to deliver a message from God. It's a glorious message of promise. God will send a Savior to the world. He will be a Light to humankind. We will know the Holy One has arrived by this sign: a virgin shall conceive and bear a son. This coming miracle has been promised by God.

Reader: A reading from the Old Testament book of the Prophet Isaiah, chapter 9, verses 2 and 6: *The people that walked in darkness have seen a great light: they that dwell in the land of the shadow of death, upon them hath the light shined. For unto us a child is born, unto us a son is given: and the government shall be upon his shoulder: and his name shall be called Wonderful Counselor, the Mighty God, the Everlasting Father, the Prince of Peace.*

Narrator 1: Unlike many of the fiery desert and wilderness prophets of the Old Testament, Isaiah was different. He was a respected statesman of Jerusalem and a royal counselor. It is interesting to note that Isaiah was *so convinced* of the events which he foretold that he often recorded his prophecies in *past tense form* as if they had already happened: "*have* seen," "*is* born," "*is* given."

(Prophets exit down the center aisle while saying the following lines to congregational members. The Prophets should walk separate from one another and can speak at the same time with their words directed toward different members.)

Micah: I have been given a message by God to deliver to you all: A Savior will come. He is coming to Bethlehem. *(Repeat as necessary)*

Isaiah: Hear the word of the Lord God. A virgin will bear a son. Hear God's word. Hear God's promise. *(Repeat as necessary)*

Narrator 2: Messages from the throne of God were not only given to prophets to deliver among men, but also to angels. The word "angel" means "messenger." Gabriel was the angel sent to deliver the announcement to the Virgin Mary that she had been chosen by God to give birth to the promised Messiah.

Reader: A reading from the Gospel of Luke, chapter 1, verses 26 and 27: *And in the sixth month the angel Gabriel was sent from God unto a city of Galilee, named Nazareth, to a virgin espoused to a man whose name was Joseph, of the house of David; and the virgin's name was Mary.*

(Mary enters front during the Bible reading above. Angel enters side after the reading and approaches Mary. Mary gasps and appears startled when she sees the Angel.)

Angel 1: Fear not, Mary, for you have found favor with God. And, behold, you will bring forth a son, and you will call his name Jesus. He will be great, and will be called the Son of the Highest. His kingdom will never end.

Mary: How can this be? I am not even married yet.

Angel 1: The Holy Spirit will come upon you, and the power of God will overshadow you.

Mary: Behold, I am the handmaid of the Lord; let it be to me according to what you have said.

(Angel exits side. Mary exits front.)

Narrator 1: Mary's response, "Behold, I am the handmaid of the Lord; let it be to me according to what you have said," was her free acceptance of this honor of honors.

Narrator 2: Mary accepted the glorious news that the Old Testament promises were about to be fulfilled. She told her future husband, Joseph, about the visit from the angel. The news that his wife-to-be was expecting a child confused him. He knew the child she carried could not be his, so he decided to part from Mary. Just then, an angel of the Lord was sent to reassure Joseph that the child was indeed holy.

(Joseph enters front and sits on a chair. He rests his head on his hand and looks troubled.)

Joseph: I don't know what to do. Mary says she was visited by an angel who told her she will give birth to the promised Messiah. I have read the scriptures. I know God's prophet, Isaiah, foretold the Savior would be born to a virgin. But ... to Mary? *(Pauses)* I just find this too hard to believe.

(Angel enters side and approaches Joseph.)

Angel 2: Joseph, fear not to take Mary for your wife, for it is true that she is carrying the Son of God. She will bear a son, and you will call him Jesus for he will save his people from their sins.

(Angel exits side. Joseph exits front.)

Narrator 1: The name Jesus was in itself a prophecy of promise, for the Hebrew meaning of the name Jesus is "He will save." This refers, of course, to our sins. Jesus was more than the name the Son of God would be called, it was what he *would do*.

Narrator 2: The prophecies in God's word told of a coming Savior. God's word is God's promise, and *(pauses and prepares to annunciate the next words)* the Promise came.

(Narrators 1 and 2 are seated as the organ begins playing the introduction to the next hymn. Narrators 3 and 4 step to the pulpit.)

Congregtional Hymn   "O Come, O Come, Emmanuel"

Scene: Bethlehem

(A Roman town crier enters from the rear of church, marching down the center aisle carrying a scroll. Before he unrolls the scroll, he holds it up high and calls loudly to the right side of the congregation while he is still near the back of church, "Hear ye." Then he holds the scroll up high again while turning to the left side of the congregation and again yells, "Hear ye." At this time the scroll is unrolled. He cries out the announcement written on the scroll. His announcement is delivered to both sides of the congregation as he continues turning from side to side. He exits out the front sanctuary door, still calling out the words of the tax order and repeating the words on the scroll at least three times.)

Roman: Hear ye! *(Pauses)* Hear ye! *(Pauses)* Caesar Augustus has ordered the world to be taxed. Everyone must go to the city of their ancestors to be enrolled. This is an order under the law. Everyone is to be taxed. *(Repeat as necessary)*

Narrator 3: This decree of Caesar Augustus was an order by the Roman government organizing a tax poll throughout the empire. This order required Joseph, the carpenter from Nazareth, to return to the city from which his ancestors had come, Bethlehem. A strenuous journey of approximately five days and covering seventy miles was now before him. Mary, being great with child, accompanied Joseph.

Narrator 4: The hand of the Lord God would protect them from harm as they traveled the necessary route between Galilee and Bethlehem which wove into hill country, an area dangerous and filled with thieves. As Mary and Joseph entered the gates of the city, little did the sleeping town of Bethlehem know that prophecy of old was about to be fulfilled within its walls.

("O Little Town Of Bethlehem" is played as a piano solo during the next Bible reading. Three Innkeepers enter from front sanctuary door, positioning themselves separate from one another; left, right, and center. Mary and Joseph enter slowly down the center aisle from the rear of the church during the Bible reading and stop at the left front of the altar. They will approach the Left Innkeeper first, the Right Innkeeper second, and the Center Innkeeper last.)

Reader: A reading from the Gospel of Luke, chapter 2, verses 1 through 6: *And it came to pass in those days that there went out a decree from Caesar Augustus, that all the world should be taxed. And this taxing was first made when Cyrenius was governor of Syria. And all went to be taxed, every one into his own city. And Joseph also went up from Galilee, out of the city of Nazareth, into Judea, unto the city of David, which is called Bethlehem, because he was of the house and lineage of David: to be taxed with Mary his espoused wife, being great with child. And so it was, that, while they were there, the days were accomplished that she should be delivered.*

Joseph: We have come to be taxed and need shelter. Do you have room?

Innkeeper 1: My inn has been full for days. I am sorry, but there is no room within.

Joseph: Please ...

Innkeeper 1: *(Firmly)* I am sorry. *(Abruptly turns and exits)*

Joseph: *(Approaches Right Innkeeper)* We have come to be taxed and need shelter. Have you any room at all?

Innkeeper 2: We have none. All of Bethlehem is full. I cannot help you.

Joseph: Please ... My wife is expecting a child this very night.

Innkeeper 2: *(Firmly)* I cannot help you. *(Abruptly turns and exits)*

Joseph: *(Approaches Center Innkeeper)* We have come to be taxed and need shelter. I beg of you, please help us. My wife ... *(Points to Mary)*

Innkeeper 3: My inn is full, but there is an animal shelter nearby. It is all I have to offer.

Joseph: Thank you for your kindness.

(Innkeeper exits front. Mary and Joseph position themselves in manger area at center altar. The manger is constructed in a house shape with crude open boards. Two bales of hay are within.)

Reader: A reading from the Gospel of Luke, chapter 2, verse 7: *And she brought forth her firstborn son, and wrapped him in swaddling clothes, and laid him in a manger.*

(The accompaniment to "Away In A Manger" begins playing immediately as the children begin to gather at the front altar area to sing. The accompaniment may be played by one of the children.)

Children's Song   "Away In A Manger"

(Children exit from front area while the accompaniment to "Away In A Manger" is played one last time to soften the movement of the children returning to their places.)

Scene: Shepherds And Angels

("It Came Upon The Midnight Clear" is played as a piano solo during the next Bible reading. Shepherds walk in during the Bible reading from all available sanctuary entrances carrying stuffed sheep and walking staffs. The Shepherds walk slowly during the instrumental music and eventually gather in the front altar area somewhat away from Mary and Joseph.)

Reader: *(Allow the music to play a short while before beginning to read.)* A reading from the Gospel of Luke, chapter 2, verses 8 through 11: *And there were in the same country shepherds abiding in the field, keeping watch over their flock by night. And, lo, the angel of the Lord came upon them, and the glory of the Lord shone round about them: and they were sore afraid.*

(All Angels — including 1 and 2 — enter side and approach Shepherds.)

Angel 3: Fear not: for, behold, I bring you good tidings of great joy, which shall be to all people. For unto you is born this day in the city of David a Savior, which is Christ the Lord.

Angel 4: Glory! Glory! Glory!

Angel 5: Glory to God in the highest!

Angel 6: Praise God!

Angel 7: And on earth peace, good will toward men!

Angel 8: And this shall be a sign to you: You will find the baby wrapped in swaddling clothes and lying in a manger.

All Angels: *(Flap arms)* Glory! Glory! Glory! Glory to God in the highest! *(Repeat as necessary)*

(When the organ begins playing the introduction to the next congregational hymn, the Angels, divided into three groups, exit down the center and side aisles. They exit flapping their arms and saying the unison words above: "Glory! Glory! Glory! Glory to God in the highest!" The Shepherds stay at the front during the hymn.)

Congregational Hymn   "Angels We Have Heard On High"

Narrator 3: Although the glorious message of Jesus' birth was delivered to the shepherds, the angels said the message of *"good* tidings and *great* joy" was for *"all* people." The angels did not announce the birth *"a baby,"* but rather announced the birth of *"a Savior."* Again the name Jesus means "he will save" and his name promised the saving forgiveness which would come through him.

Narrator 4: Scripture tells us the shepherds responded to the angels' message *"in haste."*

Shepherd 1: Let us go over to Bethlehem to see this thing that has happened, which the Lord has made known to us.

*("Hark! The Herald Angels Sing" is played as a piano instrumental solo while **all** the Shepherds "travel" to Bethlehem. The Shepherds exit down one of the side aisles and immediately return from the back of the church up the center aisle. They go over to the manger area at the front altar and kneel before the crib during the next Bible reading.)*

(The Bible reading does not begin until the carol is finished and the Shepherds have returned from their "travels to Bethlehem" and are at the front altar area once again.)

Reader: A reading from the Gospel of Luke, chapter 2, verses 15 through 20: *And it came to pass, as the angels were gone away from them into heaven, the shepherds said one to another, "Let us now go even unto Bethlehem, and see this thing which is come to pass, which the Lord hath made known unto us." And they came with haste, and found Mary, and Joseph, and the babe lying in a manger. And when they had seen it, **they made known abroad** the saying which was told them concerning this child. And all they that heard it wondered at those things which were told them by the shepherds. But Mary kept all these things, and pondered them in her heart. And the shepherds returned, glorifying and praising God for all the things that they had heard and seen, as it was told unto them.*

(Shepherds stand and face the congregation as they speak to one another.)

Shepherd 2: We must go and tell *everyone* about the glorious happenings we have seen this very night.

Shepherd 3: Yes, yes! *Everyone!* The angel *did* tell us the *"good news"* was for *"all"* men.

Shepherd 4: The world has waited for thousands of years for the promised Savior and he is finally here.

Shepherd 5: We must proclaim the good news of God's promises fulfilled.

Shepherd 6: Let us go!

*(The Shepherds go out into the congregation witnessing their experience to the audience. Two Shepherds go down each side aisle and the remaining two Shepherds go down the center aisle. They are excited **and loud**. All six Shepherds are talking at once to different people. The shepherds continue to repeat their witness to as many different congregational members as possible and eventually exit through the back of the church.)*

Shepherds 1-6: *(Any or all of the words below are said by the six shepherds. Each shepherd can go about delivering his news in whatever manner is most comfortable for him. Suggestions follow)* I am a shepherd and was watching over my flock tonight when suddenly the skies opened and angels from heaven appeared! *Angels* I tell you! It's the truth! Angels appeared *to me* and I was *just terrified* until they told me not to be afraid! They came to tell *me* and the other shepherds God's son had been born! Can you just imagine? The Savior which was promised in the Old Testament *has come*! I have seen him with *my own eyes*! I have looked upon the Salvation of the world! I have beheld his glory! The angels said that God's son could be found in Bethlehem and I traveled there and found him! Just like the angels said, he was there in Bethlehem lying in a manger! Praise God! He is come! The promise is come! Glory to God! You can find the Holy Child in Bethlehem just like I did! He is come! The Savior is come!

Narrator 3: *(With triumphant emphasis)* He is come! The Savior of the world is come!

Congregational Hymn   "Joy To The World"

(A brown sheet is placed over the open-boarded manger structure during the above hymn. The manger now looks more like a house. The two hay bales are also removed. Finally, "Baby" Jesus is exchanged for a young child approximately two years old. The three Wise Men enter up the center aisle from the rear of church during the last verse of the hymn and stand at the front altar area away from Mary and Joseph.)

Narrator 4: The Gospel of Matthew records the visit of Wise Men from the east who came to the palace of King Herod in Jerusalem seeking the One who had been born King of all kings. According to scripture, the extensive preparations and journey of these travelers took about two years.

Wise Man 1: Where is he that is born King of the Jews ...

Wise Man 2: ... for we have seen his star in the east ...

Wise Man 3: ... and have come to worship him.

Narrator 3: Using the information they obtained at King Herod's palace and looking to the heavenly star, the Wise Men were led to Bethlehem.

(The Wise Men turn to the manger area which now looks like a house and kneel before the child Jesus. They will stay in this kneeling position until the play ends.)

Reader: A reading from the Gospel of Matthew, chapter 2, verses 10 through 11: *When they saw the star, they rejoiced with exceeding great joy. And when they were come into the house, they saw the young child with Mary his mother, and fell down, and worshiped him: and when they had opened their treasures, they presented unto him gifts: gold, and frankincense, and myrrh.*

Narrator 4: Bearing gifts of gold, frankincense, and myrrh, the Wise Men fell down and worshiped the Blessed Son of God.

Narrator 3: The gift of gold symbolized Jesus as King of all kings. Frankincense — a fragrant resin placed on the temple altar by priests prior to burning sacrificed offerings — was a prophetic gift that Jesus' life would be sacrificed. Myrrh, which was an ointment used to prepare the body for burial, was also a prophetic gift that this Child was to die.

Narrator 4: Together we have gathered here to remember and rejoice in the greatest gift ever given: the gift of God's son, Jesus.

Narrator 3: We just sang "Joy to the world, the Lord is come. Let earth *receive* her King."

Narrator 4: The gift from God has been given, but as any gift, it waits *to be accepted and received.*

Narrator 3: May the gift of eternal salvation through faith in Jesus Christ the Lord fill your heart today and always.

Narrators 3 and 4: Oh, come, let us adore him.

Congregational Hymn   "Silent Night"

Organ Recessional   "Go Tell It On The Mountain"

Four Christmas Plays

Revelations Of Jesus

Given From Heaven/Received On Earth

Nativity

If It Happened Today

Mary Connealy

Contents

Introduction

Director's Notes

The Youth Narrator parts may be given to younger children who are able to read. Parts may be combined or divided to match the number of students available. There is no need for memorization of the narration parts and one brief run-through is the only required rehearsal time.

The Bible character parts should be assigned to the older children. These parts require minimal memorization. This is well within the capabilities of all children.

There are no stage sets, just one center microphone. Children enter and line up in rows, boys on one side, girls on the other. They step to the center to say their parts and then return to their rows.

For the preschool children's song, use as many pairs of little children as necessary to give all the children a part. Center the children in front before the music starts. Take all the time you need because this is nearly their whole part. Each character walks forward a few steps, stands while the verse pertaining to them is sung, and then walks back. Example: "Said the Night Wind to the Little Lamb, 'Do you see what I see?' " — Night Wind children step forward, wave their silvery arms, and then move back to the group.

Speaking Parts
12 Youth Narrators
3 Angels (or 1 to do all the Angel parts)
Mary
Joseph
Elizabeth
2 Shepherds
2 Wise Men
Simeon
Anna

Costumes

Preschool Song: Children are costumed to represent the different voices in the song "Do You Hear What I Hear?" **Night Wind:** silver ribbon, tinsel, or aluminum foil cut in strips to hang from arms, waist, and hair. This costume also needs a sign to help the audience know what it is supposed to be. **Little Lamb:** socks on hands, headband with cotton ball ears, whiskers drawn on face, black or white sweats (optional, but cute). **Shepherds and Kings:** traditional costumes.

Youth Narrators do not need special costumes, just their nice church clothes.

Bible Characters: Use traditional costumes for the Bible characters. Give Anna a cane because she is old. Make canes and shepherds' crooks by wrapping crumpled brown paper sacks around straightened wire hangers (two wrapped together at one end is a good length for crooks; one is enough for cane), tape paper on, bend top for hook.

Revelations Of Jesus

(Program And Script)

Youth 1: *(From pulpit)* Good morning *(or "evening")*. Welcome to our Christmas program. Please take a moment to stand and greet those around you and make sure to wish everyone a Merry Christmas. *(Pauses)* Now please stand and join me in singing "It Came Upon A Midnight Clear."

(Children enter during song.)

Youth 2: *(Pulpit)* Let us pray. *(Pauses to let people bow their heads)* Dear God, thank you for Christmas. Thank you for the miracle of Jesus' birth. Help us to put our faith in you. Forgive us when we fail. Help us to live our lives as Jesus would and treat everyone with love first, last, and always. In Jesus' name we pray. Amen. *(Pauses just a moment, to let the congregation know the program is starting.)*

The beginning was so simple, so tiny. The least event, a babe born in the most humble way. But his birth was like a pebble dropped into a still lake. It began a ripple that reached first one, then a dozen, then a city, a country, and the world, until today we realize that every nation marks the very existence of recorded time, from the day of Jesus' birth. Two thousand years ago Jesus was born and the ripple continues to spread, one heart at a time. This morning we celebrate this event with our Christmas program by remembering the first lives he touched. This morning we celebrate "Revelations Of Jesus."

Song   "Do You Hear What I Hear?"
(All children sing. Night Wind, Little Lambs, Shepherd Boys, and Mighty Kings come forward when their parts are sung.)

Youth 3: *(Pulpit)* The song "Do You Hear What I Hear?" is a good example of the way the news about Jesus spread. Jesus was revealed first to his mother through an angel in Luke, chapter 1, verses 26 through 36. The angel Gabriel was sent from God to a city in Galilee called Nazareth, to a virgin engaged to a man whose name was Joseph. Her name was Mary. Gabriel said,

Angel: *(Center microphone)* "Hail, favored one! The Lord is with you. Do not be afraid, for you have found favor with God. And behold, you will bear a son, and you shall name him Jesus. He will be great and will be called the Son of the Most High, and the Lord God will give him the throne of his father David; and he will reign over the house of Jacob forever; and his kingdom will have no end."

Mary: *(Center microphone)* And Mary said, "Behold, the bond slave of the Lord; be it done to me according to your word."

91

Youth 4: *(Pulpit)* Now one person on earth knows of Jesus. The pebble makes its first, almost silent, splash into the water of time. *(Long pause during which Joseph lays down beside the center microphone)* Jesus was revealed next to his earthly father, Joseph, in Matthew, chapter 1, verses 20 through 24. Behold an angel of the Lord appeared to him in a dream, saying,

Angel: *(Waves her hand over Joseph sleeping on floor)* "Joseph, son of David, do not be afraid to take Mary as your wife. She will bear a son; and you shall call his name Jesus, for it is he who will save his people from their sins."

Joseph: *(Gets up; center microphone)* Joseph arose from his sleep, and did as the angel of the Lord commanded him and took Mary as his wife. Now two people on earth know of Jesus' holiness. The first ripple begins to spread outward, still too tiny for the world to see.

Youth 5: *(Pulpit)* Jesus was revealed next to Elizabeth in Luke, chapter 1, verses 41 through 43, when she was expecting her own son, John, who would grow up to be a mighty servant of God. Elizabeth heard Mary greet her and Elizabeth's baby leaped in her womb; and Elizabeth was filled with the Holy Spirit. And she cried out,

Elizabeth: *(To Mary, both at center microphone)* "Blessed among women are you, and blessed is the fruit of your womb! And how has it happened to me, that the mother of my Lord should come to me? For behold, when the sound of your greeting reached my ears, the baby in my womb leaped for joy."

Youth 6: *(Pulpit)* A third person joins in the spreading circle and a fourth because the unborn baby, John the Baptist, knew Jesus. Elizabeth would certainly have told her husband Zechariah and he was a priest. He might have preached about this revelation and told hundreds more, but he could not speak. An angel revealed to him the news that even though he and his wife were very old, they would have a son. For months his tongue had been silenced for his lack of faith. So again the word spreads, but slowly.

Youth 7: *(Pulpit)* He was revealed to the shepherds in the fields on the night of his birth in Luke, chapter 2, verses 8 through 20. "And in the same region there were some shepherds staying out in the fields, and keeping watch over their flock by night. And an angel of the Lord suddenly stood before them and the glory of the Lord shone around them; and they were terribly frightened. And the angel said to them,

Angel: *(Center microphone)* "Do not be afraid; for behold, I bring you good news of a great joy which shall be for all the people; for today in the city of David there has been born for you a Savior, who is Christ the Lord. And this will be a sign for you; you will find a baby wrapped in cloths and lying in a manger."

Youth 7: *(Pulpit)* Suddenly there appeared with the angel a multitude of the heavenly host praising God, saying,

All Children: *(Speak together loudly)* "Glory to God in the highest, and on earth peace among men with whom he is pleased."

Youth 7: *(Pulpit)* And it came about when the angels had gone away from them into heaven, that the shepherds began saying to one another,

Shepherd 1: *(Center microphone, talking to little boys dressed like Shepherds)* "Let us go straight to Bethlehem then, and see this thing that has happened which the Lord has made known to us." And they came in haste and found their way to Mary and Joseph, and the baby as he lay in the manger. And when they had seen this, they made known the statement which had been told them about this Child. And all who heard it wondered at the things which were told them by the shepherds.

Mary: *(Center microphone)* But Mary treasured all these things, pondering them in her heart.

Shepherd 2: *(Center microphone)* And the shepherds went back, glorifying and praising God for all that they had heard and seen, just as had been told them. In verse 18 the Bible says, "All who heard wondered at the things which were told them by the shepherd." Now how many know? How far has the news spread? To a dozen, maybe to a hundred?

Youth 8: *(Pulpit)* Jesus was revealed to the Wise Men in Matthew, chapter 2, verses 1 through 12. "Now after Jesus was born in Bethlehem of Judea, in the days of Herod the king, behold, magi from the east arrived in Jerusalem, saying,

Wise Man 1: *(Center microphone)* "Where is he who has been born King of the Jews? For we saw his star in the east, and have come to worship him." Now the news of Jesus has reached, through a heavenly sign, far distant lands.

Wise Man 2: *(Center microphone)* When the Wise Men returned to their own countries they must have taken the news of what they had seen with them, spreading the word of Jesus' birth far and wide and preparing hearts for what is to come.

Song   "Jesus, Name Above All Names"
(Older girls singing group)   *(The Kids Praise Album* © 1980,
                                                              Maranatha Music, Laguna Hills, California)

Youth 9: *(Pulpit)* Jesus is revealed to Herod in Matthew, chapter 2, through the words of the Wise Men. Herod spreads the news when he consults his chief priests and scribes. It is interesting that a revelation of Jesus possibly had the most powerful impact on the one truly evil man who heard the news. In chapter 2, verse 16, the Bible says, "Herod became enraged and sent and slew all the male children who were in Bethlehem and in all its environs, from two years old and under, according to the time which he had ascertained from the magi." Herod's act of brutality revealed Jesus' power by revealing Herod's fear of him. It is possible that this monstrous deed may have spread the news of Jesus more than any other event because surely everyone heard about this terrible slaughter and wanted to know why.

Youth 10: *(Pulpit)* Jesus was revealed to Simeon in Luke, chapter 2, verses 25 through 35. "And behold, there was a man in Jerusalem whose name was Simeon; and this man was righteous and devout, looking for the consolation of Israel and the Holy Spirit was upon him. And it had been revealed to him by the Holy Spirit that he would not see death before he had seen the Lord's Christ. And he came in the Spirit into the temple; and when the parents brought in the child Jesus, to carry out for him the custom of the Law; then Simeon took him into his arms and blessed God, and said,

Simeon: *(Center microphone)* "Now, Lord, I can die content! For I have seen him as you promised me I would. I have seen the Savior you have given to the world. He is the Light that will shine upon the nations, and he will be the glory of your people Israel."

Youth 10: *(Pulpit)* And his father and mother were amazed at the things which were being said about him. And Simeon blessed them, and said to Mary, his mother,

Simeon: "A sword shall pierce your soul, for this child shall be rejected by many in Israel, and this to their undoing. But he will be the greatest joy of many others. And the deepest thoughts of many hearts shall be revealed."

Youth 10: Now a man, righteous and devout, has added his voice to those who believe that God has sent salvation in the form of this little baby. Jesus is revealed to Simeon by the Holy Spirit. Even now, when Jesus is but eight days old, Simeon sees salvation for Israel and for all the Gentiles. A Gentile means anyone who is not Jewish; that means Jesus is for the whole world.

Youth 11: *(Pulpit)* He was revealed to Anna in Luke, chapter 2, verses 36 through 38.

Anna: *(Center microphone)* "And there was a prophetess, Anna. She was advanced in years. She never left the temple, serving night and day with fasting and prayers. She came up to the baby Jesus and began giving thanks to God. She continued to speak of Jesus to all those who were looking for the redemption of Jerusalem." Jesus is only eight days old, and already, because of Anna and Simeon, Jesus has been revealed to hundreds.

Youth 11: And the child continued to grow and become strong. The grace of God was upon him. Jesus increased in wisdom and stature and in the favor of God and men. He is a child. He has thirty years to wait before he preaches a single word. But already the world is being prepared. Already the ripples have spread across the waiting world. Seeds are being sown. The word continues to spread today from the people who *are* God's children to the people who *will be* God's children.

Song   "Children Of The Lord" (*The Kids Praise Album*)
(Small group or all children)   or "O Come, All Ye Faithful"

Youth 12: *(Pulpit)* Please join me in prayer. *(Pauses to let people bow their heads)* Dear Lord, thank you for your son Jesus. Help us spread the word. Thank you for letting us be part of the wide circle of believers. Thank you for Christmas, God. Thank you for this chance to celebrate the day that Jesus was sent into the world. Amen. *(Pauses)*

As you enjoy the fun of Christmas, the gifts, the food, the reunions, may the peace of God be with you all until we meet again. May you know the love and joy that come from accepting Christ as your Savior. May your Christmas spirit truly be a holy one. And, with your own life, may you be a part of the *Revelation of Jesus*. Now please join in singing "The First Noel." *(Children exit)*

94

Introduction

Director's Notes

All four speakers speak from the pulpit; their parts do not need to be memorized. Use youth group members to include them in the program or give these parts to elementary children if you need more roles for this age. My time-honored tradition for narrator roles is to give them to the most unruly children; then give those children permission to miss all the rehearsals except for the final run-through at the last minute. You have to be sure they can pronounce all the words. One person can do all the narration if you are short of children.

Angels have boys' names, but they *do not* have to be boys. Change the names if a girl doesn't like being called Elijah. Gabriel can be a girl's name and the Archangel can be a girl. Only Noah has a role (Rain Expert) that is identified as connected with the Bible, although David's leading the music is a nice touch. This play requires little memorization. (Example — Isaiah has only five short lines; David, four; Elijah, three; plus several lines all angels say together, like "What!" but remembering *when* to say them takes some rehearsal.)

Speaking Parts
4 Speakers
6 Angels (Isaiah, Noah, Gabriel, David, Archangel, Elijah)
God
3 Wise Men
Mary
Shepherd

Costumes

The costumes are traditional: Angels wear angel robes and wings and circles of garland that just set on their heads for haloes. God wears an angel robe with no wings.

Props

Sign saying "Given From Heaven," sign saying "Received On Earth," big silver star on a long stick, bucket with removable poster paper cloud taped on side and containing a handful of tinsel, halo (circle of silver or gold garland) on string for Gabriel, and cover for God to be folded into "baby" (white or plain colored baby blanket or cloth).

Sets

Chairs in back of stage on left and right side for Gabriel to stand on and yell and for two Wise Men to stand on. Chair in center back for Elijah to stand on and hold up star. If you want to include a stable, use a big cardboard box. Cover stable with blue sheet with clouds on it for First Scene, then remove blue sheet to show stable for Second Scene.

Have Shepherds, Wise Men, littlest children sit in chairs in front or in choir loft during the first scene, or have children play two parts. There can be more Angels than there are speaking parts, but if your Second Scene Shepherds are First Scene Angels this will require a costume change.

Given From Heaven/Received On Earth

(Program And Script)

Speaker 1: There was joy and excitement in heaven on Christmas Eve. Although the earth slept below, unaware of the approach of the greatest moment of history, in heaven all was in readiness. How different the two places were that long ago night. We would like now to present our play "Given From Heaven/Received On Earth." Please join me in singing "There's A Song In The Air." *(Know hymn number)*

(Children enter during song. Two Angels enter from the side carrying a sign that says, "Given From Heaven.")

Speaker 1: And now part one of our play.

Scene One

(Opening is an explosion of noise and motion to contrast with opening of Scene Two. Angels rush around getting haloes on and adjusting wings and clothing. Chaotic! Older students help younger ones. Say all the first six lines jumbled up, on top of each other. The children bump into each other, use the whole stage, repeat their lines several times, or say someone else's lines, generally making a lot of noise! Make sure Gabriel can be heard. His halo hangs by a string down his back. He spins around as he is looking for his halo so people notice the halo.)

Angel 1 (Isaiah): Hurry! Hurry!
Angel 2 (Noah): We can't be late.
Angel 3 (Gabriel): I can't find my halo!
Angel 4 (David): Help me get this on, please!
Angel 5 (Archangel): Hurry up! Hurry up, everybody!
Angel 6 (Elijah): Are my wings on straight?

Gabriel: *(Stands on chair at back of stage or on choir pews and yells)* Where's my halo?

(One speaker at a time, but still urgent, still getting dressed.)

Isaiah: We have to be ready. Could you believe that guy wouldn't let them have a room in his inn?

Noah: What a creep!

Gabriel: *(Stands on chair on opposite side of the stage, swings around so halo flies out, yells in a panic. No one pays attention to him)* Who took my halo?

96

David: Polish your haloes. We have to look perfect. *(To Noah)* Come on, you know God's had that inn filled for tonight since the creation of the earth.

Noah: Yeah, well he was still a creep!

Archangel: Practice the song if you have time. How about poor Joseph? He's been walking all over town looking for a room, when from the very beginning it was hopeless.

(Everyone should be dressed by now, except Gabriel's halo is still missing.)

God: *(Enters from side; speaks loudly but **is** happy and kind)* Nothing about tonight is hopeless. Tonight is the most hope-filled night of all time.

All Angels: *(Yell together)* Yay! *(Clap and cheer. Gabriel is back with the group, still no halo)*

God: Are you all ready?

Gabriel: *(Sheepishly)* Well — uh — I can't find my halo.

All Angels: *(Turn toward Gabriel and yell)* What!

(Gabriel turns to face Angel group, his back to the congregation. His halo is hanging down his back. Archangel puts it on his head, and turns Gabriel around. Hold for laughter.)

Archangel: We are ready in every way, God.

God: May I hear the song, please? David, will you conduct?

David: *(To congregation or children can sing alone)* Please join us in singing "Angels We Have Heard On High." *(Needs to know hymn number)*

God: That is a beautiful song and I bless you.

All Angels: Thank you, God. *(Fall to their knees and bow their foreheads all the way to the floor, very quietly, solemnly)*

God: Now I have some last minute things to do. *(Angels rise when God starts talking)* Those sheep won't settle in for the night, so the shepherds can't get to their campfire.

Gabriel: How do you make sheep go to sleep? Do they count people?

God: Elijah, get ready to light the star on Archie's signal.

Isaiah: *(Points down)* Mary and Joseph are in the stable.

Noah: They are so alone. Heaven is vibrating with the joy of this night and Earth is asleep.

God: In more ways than one. *(Exits)*

Archangel: Elijah, do you have the star ready?

Elijah: *(From back of stage, far from microphone, yells loudly)* Ready!

Isaiah: Someone go check those astrologers.

David: *(Points)* The one in Persia is awake and gazing up just like every night.

(Wise Man 1 stands on same chair Gabriel stood on, left side.)

Gabriel: *(Points)* I see the Mongolian Wise Man. He's paying attention.

(Wise Man 2 stands on Gabriel's chair on right side. Wise Man 3 enters and sits on front of stage and lays his head down, as if he's sleeping.)

Archangel: The Wise Man in China has fallen asleep! Quick, Noah, you are on rain detail. Douse him and wake him up!

Noah: Okay, but I think I'll sleet him instead. *(Holds up bucket with a cloud taped on the side)*

Isaiah: *(Frantically)* No, no! No cloud! It will block his view of the star!

Noah: *(Acts shocked, indignant)* I can't do rain or sleet without clouds! It's just not done!

Archangel: *(Firmly)* No clouds, Noah!

Noah: Look, I know about rain. There has to be a cloud!

All Angels: *(Yell at Noah)* No clouds!

Noah: *(Shrugs and pulls cloud off bucket. Tosses it carelessly aside)* Okay, but it's not done! *(Throws the tinsel. Hold for laughter)*

Wise Man 3: *(Jumps up and yells when it hits him. If people laugh a lot, he mutters and snorts around until they quiet down before saying his line)* Hey! It can't sleet, there's not a cloud in the sky!

Noah: I know how you feel, buddy.

(Wise Man 3 brushes tinsel off and storms off to right side. Stands with arms crossed, looks mad.)

Noah: *(Worried)* Gee, he's mad. *(Changes tones, perky)* But he's ready.

98

Archangel: The shepherds are sitting down finally. The Wise Men are alert! Mary and Joseph are in the stable. Our song is perfectly ready. What else? What's left?

God: *(Enters)* All that's left is for me to go.

Angels: *(Surround God, speak separately, on top of each other's words)* Good-bye. Peace on Earth. Glory to you, Lord.

God: *(Goes to pulpit and reads if memorization is difficult, because it's an important moment in the play and stepping apart emphasizes it)* I go now to take the form of a baby. I will accept all of life's joy and pain. There will be great glory in living an earthly life exactly as it should be lived. I am ready now. I know there is a lot that I will have to bear. I will do it and prove for all time that life is wonderful. That heaven begins on Earth. That the very best of life can come from any man. Even one born in a smelly, dirty barn, who dies a painful death as a criminal. I will live, I will die, and I will be raised up to life again, so all may have eternal life. I bless you all this joyous night.

All Angels: *(Bow low — same as before)* Thank you, Lord.

(God sits curled up on top step near the pulpit, head down, arms wrapped around knees. Angels cover him with small white blanket or cloth and step away from him.)

Archangel: Angels ready?

All Angels: *(All line up, except Elijah who is in the back with star, and yell)* Yes!

Archangel: Elijah, is the star ready?

Elijah: Yes!

Isaiah: *(Points down and yells)* And Mary is ready, too!

(Angels go to sit in choir loft. If necessary, they change into Shepherd or Wise Men costumes. Wise Men stay where they are, two on chairs in back and one in front off to the right. Elijah is in back center sitting on chair waiting with the star. Mary and Joseph are in front pew waiting until now [unless they're angels]. Remove cover from stable. Mary and Joseph walk to it and sit down on front of stage. Joseph lies down to sleep. Mary is sitting up quietly. Shepherds stand in front left. God is still sitting on stage covered. Don't let Shepherds stand in front of him.)

Scene Two

Speaker 2: *(Begins to read while Scene Two is set)* We have seen how all was prepared in heaven for the gift to be given. Now let us see how it was received on earth. Mary sits alone, as she sat alone when the angel came to her and told her of the baby. Joseph may have been sleeping, but even if he was awake, it is just the two of them against the world. Mary has pondered in her heart all these months the meaning of the child she will have. She is a simple, young girl; her only gift mentioned in the Bible is her faithfulness to God. Now her time is at hand and all she has seen and heard will be realized on this lonely night.

Mary: *(Rises; speaks into microphone)* My soul magnifies the Lord and my spirit rejoices in God my Savior. For he had regarded the low estate of his handmaiden, for behold all generations shall call me blessed, for he who is mighty has done great things for me and Holy is his name.

Speaker 3: *(Very solemnly, meaningfully)* Now in silence, alone, unknown to the world comes the most profound moment in history. Prophecies for thousands of years before foretold of this event. All the calendars of the world mark his birth as the center of time. We now present the rest of our play, "Received On Earth."

(Shepherds and Wise Men hold up sign: "Received On Earth.")

Speaker 3: *(To congregation — know hymn number)* Please join me in singing "Silent Night."

(After the song is a very special moment in the play. Give it plenty of time. If possible, even darken the room and use a spotlight on Mary and God. After the singing, a flute or piano should play once more through "Silent Night," while Mary walks to God and slowly, gently pulls cover off him and folds cover until it's small, then holds it in her arms like it's a baby. This should be done slowly, gracefully, almost like a dance. Mary could even spin around with cover flying out before it's folded. After it is folded she should hug it close. Bounce it gently, pretend to talk to baby, anything like that to indicate she'd has her baby and it is God transformed.)

Mary: *(After music ends, looks up at sky)* Thank you, God. *(Turns to Joseph and awakens him. He looks lovingly at the "baby" in her arms)*

God: *(Gets up, looks at couple, so loving, so alone)* Thank you, Mary. *(Exits)*

Archangel: *(Raises arms, yells. Change pace from previous solemn quiet)* It is the fullness of time!

(Elijah raises star.)

Wise Men: *(Jump up and point at star Elijah holds)* The star! What can it mean? Wow! Oh! Look! *(Excitedly, have each of them say several of the lines, talking all at once)*

Gabriel: *(Walks over to the Shepherds. Very loud proclamation)* Do not be afraid! For behold, I bring you good news which will be a joy to all people. For tonight is born to you, in the city of David, a Savior which is Christ the Lord. And this will be a sign to you. You will find a babe wrapped in swaddling clothes and lying in a manger.

All Angels: *(Sing chorus of "Angels We Have Heard On High" to the Shepherds. Angels move off to the right side of Mary. Leave room for Wise Men coming soon)*

Shepherd: Let us go to Bethlehem and see this wonderful thing that the Lord has made known to us. *(Move to left side, gathered around Mary on the side away from Angels)*

(All Wise Men gather on right side of Mary, in front of Angels.)

Wise Man 1: We have seen the star in the east.

Wise Man 2: We come with gifts of gold, frankincense, and myrrh.

Wise Man 3: We have come to worship the one who will be crowned King of the Jews.

Speaker 4: *(Speaks very clearly, slowly)* In the beginning was the Word, and the Word was with God and the Word was God. In him was life and the life was the light of men. The light shines in the darkness and the darkness has not overcome it.

The true light that enlightens every man was coming into the world. He came to his own home and his own received him not. But to all who received him, who believed in his name, he gave power to become children of God.

And the Word became flesh and dwelt among us, full of grace and truth. We have beheld his glory, glory as of the only Son from the Father. And from his fullness we have received grace upon grace. *(Pauses for moment of silence)*

Please, join me in singing "Joy To The World." *(Know hymn number. Children exit)*

Introduction

Director's Notes

Twelve speaking parts for older children can be divided or combined. Four speaking parts for preschool children. Have pairs of children saying parts so everyone gets one. Line children up in front, boys on one side, girls on the other, and have them come to one center microphone for their part, then return to their row.

Speaking Parts

12 Speakers (older children)
4 Speakers (younger children)

Costumes

Traditional costumes are used. Dress preschool children in Angel, Shepherd, and Wise Men costumes.

If desired, older children may dress in costume for the biblical part they are assigned.
Speaker 4 — Mary
Speaker 8 — Angel
Speaker 9 — Shepherd
Speaker 10 — Wise Man
Speaker 11 — Wise Man

Props

None required, other than a microphone.

Sets

None required.

Nativity
(Program And Script)

Speaker 1: Please stand and join us in singing "O Come, All Ye Faithful."

(Children enter during the song.)

Speaker 1: Welcome to our Sunday School Christmas Program. Please take a moment to greet those around you and make sure to wish them a Merry Christmas. *(Pauses)*

Before we begin our program, please bow your heads and join me in a word of prayer.

Dear Lord, help us to praise you with our program tonight and with our lives all year long. We ask for our daily bread and you give us a feast. We ask for forgiveness and you make us your children, heirs to heaven with your Son, Jesus. Help us to be worthy, Lord. Help us to keep the spirit of Christmas, which is the Holy Spirit, alive all year long. Amen.

Speaker 2: In those days Caesar Augustus issued a decree that a census should be taken of the entire Roman world. This was the first census that took place while Quirinius was governor of Syria. And everyone went to his own town to register.

So Joseph also went up from the town of Nazareth in Galilee to Judea, to Bethlehem the town of David, because he belonged to the house and line of David. He went there to register with Mary, who was pledged to be married to him and was expecting a child.

Speaker 3: The first event on that Christmas Eve so long ago was the arrival of the Holy Family in Bethlehem. The fullness of Mary's time had come — the great revelation that her son was to be the Son of God and that she was a chosen vessel of God. She had all these months remembered and pondered the angel's message and Elizabeth's greeting during the visit in the hill country in Judea.

Speaker 4: My soul magnifies the Lord and my spirit rejoices in God my Savior. For he has regarded the low estate of his handmaiden, for behold all generations shall call me blessed, for he who is mighty has done great things for me and holy is his name.

Speaker 5: The next event was the birth. It is the event on which all history turns. Jesus was born, alone in a stable with only his mother and father to attend. This fulfilled the prophecy from thousands of years before: "A virgin shall conceive and bear a son, and she shall call his name 'Emmanuel' which means: 'God with us.'"

Speaker 6: While they were there, the time came for the baby to be born, and she gave birth to her firstborn, a son. She wrapped him in cloths and placed him in a manger, because there was no room for them in the inn.

Song   "Emmanuel," "Silent Night," or "It Came Upon A Midnight Clear"
(All children sing)

Speaker 7: Next came the appearance of the angels to a few shepherds, faithful men in the field who believed the prophecies and who had prepared their hearts. The angels came down before them and were of such great number that they filled the sky.

Speaker 8: And there were shepherds living out in the fields nearby, keeping watch over their flocks at night. An angel of the Lord appeared to them, and the glory of the Lord shone around them, and they were terrified. But the angel said to them, "Do not be afraid. I bring you good news of great joy that will be for all people. Today in the town of David a Savior has been born to you, he is Christ the Lord. This will be a sign to you, you will find a baby wrapped in cloths and lying in a manger."

Suddenly a great company of the heavenly host appeared with the angel, praising God and saying, "Glory to God in the highest, and on earth peace to men in whom his favor rests."

Speaker 9: When the angels had left them and gone into heaven, the shepherds said to one another, "Let's go to Bethlehem and see this thing that has happened, which the Lord has told us about."

So they hurried off and found Mary and Joseph, and the baby, who was lying in the manger. When they had seen him, they spread the word concerning what had been told them about this child and all who heard it were amazed at what the shepherds said to them. But Mary treasured up all these things and pondered them in her heart. The shepherds returned, glorifying and praising God for all the things they had heard and seen, which were just as they had been told.

Song
(Have girls lead and sing echo on chorus.)

"While By Our Sheep" (arrangement © 1979, Singspiration, found in *Praise! Our Songs And Hymns,* Zondervan, Grand Rapids, Michigan)

1. **(all)** While by our sheep we watched that night, glad tidings brought an angel bright.
Chorus

(girls) How great our joy!	**(echo boys)** How great our joy!
Joy! Joy! Joy!	Joy! Joy! Joy!
Praise ye the Lord in heaven on high.	Praise ye the Lord in heaven on high.

2. **(all)** There shall be born so he did say, in Bethlehem today.
Chorus

(girls) How great our joy	**(echo boys)** How great our joy!
Joy! Joy! Joy!	Joy! Joy! Joy!
Praise ye the Lord in heaven on high.	Praise ye the Lord in heaven on high.

3. **(all)** There shall the child lie in a stall, this child who shall redeem us all.
Chorus

(girls) How great our joy!	**(echo boys)** How great our joy!
Joy! Joy! Joy!	Joy! Joy! Joy!
Praise ye the Lord in heaven on high.	Praise ye the Lord in heaven on high.

Speaker 10: In far-off nations, Wise Men, studying the sky, saw the appearance of a new star, brighter than all others. They were men chosen of God because of their search for truth. When they saw the star, they knew either from revelation or from knowledge of Jewish scripture that the King of the Jews was born. They proceeded at once with gifts, to pay homage to the new king.

Speaker 11: After Jesus was born in Bethlehem in Judea, during the time of King Herod, Magi from the east came to Jerusalem and asked, "Where is the one who has been born King of the Jews? We saw his star in the east and have come to worship him."

The chief priests replied, "In Bethlehem, for this is what the prophet has written." The Magi went on their way, and the star they had seen in the east went ahead of them until it stopped over the place where the child was. When they saw the star, they were overjoyed. On coming to the house, they saw the child with his mother Mary, and they bowed down and worshiped him. Then they opened their treasures and presented him with gifts of gold and of incense and of myrrh.

Song   "One Small Child"
(Great Christmas Songs For God's Kids
© 1994 Singleton Productions, Inc.,
Word Records and Music, Nashville, Tennessee)

Preschool Section
(Children speak phrases from "The First Noel." Have them in costume.)
    Angel: The first Noel the angels did say
    Shepherd: was to certain poor shepherds in fields where they lay
    Wise Man: Wise Men looked up and saw a star
    Wise Man: And by that light they came from afar.

Song   "The First Noel"
(All children sing)

Speaker 12: This concludes our Christmas program. Thank you for coming tonight. At all of your Christmas parties, through the whole season, remember to celebrate the birth of Jesus. Remember to lift high the name of Christ. Remember Bethlehem and a little baby in a manger who became the cornerstone of a whole new world. Spread the Good News about Jesus and allow the joy of Lord to lift up your whole life.

Now please stand and join us in singing "Joy To The World." *(Know hymn number)*

(Children sing first verse and then begin to exit, youngest first.)

Introduction

Director's Notes

This program has speaking parts for 33 children, including 14 youth narrators. Parts can be combined or split to accommodate fewer or more young people.

Ask parents to assist with costuming with small groups of children before the program. Some parents aren't willing to take on a big job, but most will agree to one simple, clearly-defined task. Have a parent for each scene if possible, so in practice the children can split up and all practice at the same time. This helps control unruly children by keeping them busy, separating them, and having their parents around. It also helps parents realize children need to learn their lines.

Youth group children do all readings. Combine or divide readings so everyone has a part. Parts are not memorized, and need almost no rehearsal. Substitute group songs if small groups aren't willing to sing. Surprisingly many children like the idea of an "almost" solo.

Tell the children to *hold for laughs*. Their words cannot be heard over laughter.

Running time is about 30 minutes.

We added to the impact of this program in our church by naming the characters after members of the congregation. Example: We didn't call Jesus' mother "Mary," we called her by the child's real name. In the Innkeeper and Joseph scene, we made a sign bearing the name of a real business and added "and Inn — No Vacancies." We used KB Lawn Service and Inn because the father of the child who played the Innkeeper owned that business. We also tried to match children to characters with their parents' or grandparents' names. The Wise Man and Wife were named for local farmers; the boy who played the Wise Man was their grandson. The wording about "spraying" was a farming reference; you should substitute an activity that matches the career you choose. The girl in the Shepherd's scene played the character named for her own mother. References to Bethlehem in the scenes could be changed to your town or your neighborhood or church. The idea is to personalize the events surrounding Jesus' birth and make people think about the way people reacted to the news about Jesus.

One final note: Because I mentioned people in our congregation by name I made sure to **get permission** before doing this. I gave them the scene that referred to them, and I explained that their child or grandchild would be playing them. I pointed out that even though "they" might say something silly in the play, in the end they rose to the call of God and in fact were heroic. Everyone was very nice about it and I believe it actually created some interest, but I didn't want to surprise them in case someone thought he or she was being made fun of.

Costumes

Angel outfits: Angel appears in several scenes. One child can be the angel or several, depending on how many children need a role. Angel has a wand she whacks people with (the angels are tough and funny and *very* bossy). In Scene Five, Angel produces a yellow cardboard lightning bolt; make it huge so people can see it. Expect laughter.

Scene Six: Shepherds use two cell phones, four cardboard sheep suspended from belt loops with string. Children dressed in flannel shirts and baseball caps.

Scene Seven: Wise Man and Wife use two cell phones, a tractor made with cardboard and hung by suspenders or string from child's shoulders (easily lowered over the head of the Wise Man.)

Props

Three folding chairs, angel wand (stick with star and tinsel dangling), cardboard sign for inn, yellow lightning bolt (3 feet long, one foot wide, made of cardboard), two cell phones, four cardboard sheep, cardboard tractor, cardboard or posterboard stars on string to hang on "Stars" in little children's parts.

Sets

The entire set required is three folding chairs — to sit in for Scenes Two and Three, as a bed in Scene Four, and as a counter and a place to hang the sign at the inn in Scene Five.

In the following pages of script, wherever the name of one of the Bible characters appears as a noun of address in the dialogue, your actors should say the name of the child playing the biblical character or the name of the child's parent or grandparent, as appropriate. These nouns of address are indicated with bold italics.

If It Happened Today

(Program And Script)

(Young person plays piano or instrumental prelude.)

Youth 1: Good morning. *(Pauses for congregational response of "Good morning")* Welcome to our Christmas Program "If It Happened Today." Please stand and greet the people around you and wish them a Merry Christmas. *(Pauses for greeting)*

(Pastor does offering and prayers. Then play resumes.)

Youth 2: Everyone please stand and sing verses 1, 2, and 3 of "Hark! The Herald Angels Sing."

(Children enter during hymn.)

Youth 2: We begin our program by remembering that Christmas night so long ago, how it was, how the angels sang and the shepherds and Wise Men came. And how a star shone bright to lead the way.

Preschool/Kindergarten Participation
(Children in position; prompt them. Each one stands in front of microphone. Use several angels, shepherds, and so on for each part if necessary to give each child a part, or have one child do several parts.)

Angel (Child 1): Angels sang about his birth.
Wise Man (Child 2): Wise Men sought and found him.
Big Star (Child 3): Heaven's star shone brightly forth.
Big Star (Child 4): Glory all around him.
Shepherd (Child 5): Shepherds saw the wondrous sight,
Angel (Child 6): Beautiful the story.
Angel (Child 7): Praise his name in all the earth.
Angel (Child 8): Hail! The King of Glory!

Youth 3: All those years ago Jesus came into the world and he is with us still. We are called as believers to spread the Good News, believe the testimony of Jesus' family, the shepherds, and the Wise Men. We are all called upon to be faithful. To be joyful. To be triumphant. To come and adore Christ the Lord.

Song   "O Come, All Ye Faithful"
(Older girls sing as indicated below)
1. **(duet)** O come, all ye faithful,
Joyful and triumphant.
O come ye, o come ye to Bethlehem.

108

Come and behold him, born the King of Angels,
O come, let us adore him.
(add more voices) O come, let us adore him.
(all) O come, let us adore him, Christ the Lord.

2. **(duet, different girls)** Sing choirs of angels.
Sing in exultation.
Sing all ye citizens of heaven above.
Glory to God all glory in the highest.
O come, let us adore him.
(add more voices) O come, let us adore him.
(all) O come, let us adore him, Christ the Lord.

3. **(all)** Yea, Lord, we greet thee!
Born this happy morning!
Jesus to thee be all glory given!
Word of the Father now in flesh appearing!
(duet) O come, let us adore him.
(add more voices) O come, let us adore him.
(all) O come let us adore him, Christ the Lord.
(all) O come, let us adore him, Christ the Lord.

Youth 4: Jesus came into the world 2,000 years ago. He came to faithful people who awaited the coming of a Savior. People like us. We don't know how these people reacted when angels started talking to them, but it is most likely, just like now, an angel appearing and talking was a very unusual occurrence. We wondered how we at the *(name of your church)* would act *(Pauses)* "If It Happened Today."

Youth 5:   Luke 1:26-38
    In the sixth month, God sent the angel Gabriel to Nazareth, a town in Galilee, to a virgin pledged to be married to a man named Joseph, a descendant of David. The virgin's name was Mary. The angel went to her and said, "Greetings, you who are highly favored! The Lord is with you!"
    Mary was greatly troubled at these words and wondered what kind of greeting this might be. But the angel said to her, "Do not be afraid, Mary, you have found favor with God. You will be with child and give birth to a son, and you are to give him the name Jesus. He will be great and will be called the Son of the Most High. The Lord God will give him the throne of his father David, and he will reign over the house of Jacob forever. His kingdom will never end."
    "How will this be," Mary asked the angel, "since I am a virgin?"
    The angel answered, "The Holy Spirit will come upon you and the power of the Most High will overshadow you. So the holy one to be born will be called the Son of God. Even Elizabeth your relative is going to have a child in her old age and she who was said to be barren is in her sixth month. For nothing is impossible with God."
    "I am the Lord's servant," Mary answered. "May it be to me as you have said." Then the angel left her.
    (Pauses for a moment; looks out at people) That's how it happened then. If it happened today ...

109

Scene One: Angel Telling Mary

Angel: *(Waving wand)* Peace be with you! The Lord is with you and has greatly blessed you!

(Mary covers her face and bows her head — acts afraid.)

Angel: Fear not, **MARY**! God has been gracious to you. You are going to have a baby. You will give birth to a son, and you will name him Jesus. He will be called the Son of the Most High God. The Lord God will make him a king, as his ancestor David was, and he will be the king of the descendants of Jacob forever; his kingdom will never end.

Mary: I'm not married. How can I have a child?

Angel: Your baby will be a miracle just as your cousin Elizabeth's baby is a miracle. There is nothing God cannot do.

Mary: What will my parents say?

Angel: Trust God, **MARY**. He will prepare their hearts.

Mary: What will **JOSEPH** say?

Angel: Trust God for all your worries.

Mary: I am the Lord's servant. I accept the Lord's will.

Scene Two: Mary And Her Parents

Mary: *(Walks up steps, sounds worried)* Mom, Dad, come in here. I've got something to tell you.

(Mary's parents enter.)

Angel: *(Comes in from behind Mary's parents. She rests her hands on both their shoulders. No one sees her or feels her)* Trust **MARY**.

Mary: *(Sits down on chair opposite two chairs together)* I think you'd better sit down.

Mary's Mother: What is it, **MARY**? *(Sits down in one of the two chairs together, opposite Mary)*

Mary's Father: *(Impatiently)* Can this wait until later? I need to finish what I'm doing.

Mother: Sit down, *(insert name of child cast as Mary)*. Can't you see it's important?

(Father sits beside Mother, with arms crossed. Angel follows them, keeping her hands on their backs.)

Mary: I want you to listen to my whole story before you say anything. It's going to be a shock, but an angel came into my room and talked to me.

Father: An angel!

Mother: *(Stands up)* **MARY**, I don't have time for your jokes. I need to get dinner on.

Angel: *(Keeps her hand on Mother's shoulder as she rises)* Trust God. Trust your daughter.

Father: Sit down and let her finish, *(insert name of mother of child cast as Mary)*.

(Mother sits down again.)

Mary: There's no easy way to say this. The angel told me God has chosen me for a very special purpose. She said I am greatly blessed! I'm ... *(Hesitates)* I'm going to have a baby.

Mother: *(Stands up fast and yells)* A baby! No! It's not true!

Father: *(Stands up and says angrily)* Where is **JOSEPH**! Wait until I get my hands on him!

Mother: We'll have to move! We can never live this down!

Father: An angel, of all things. I'm ashamed of you, MARY, for making an excuse like that!

Mary: *(Yells over their lines so loudly they're shocked)* Listen to me!

Angel: *(Slaps both of them on the back of their heads)* Trust MARY!

(Mother and Father react to the blow but they turn around and look right at the Angel and don't see her.)

Mary: Sit down, both of you!

(Mother and Father sit.)

Mary: *(Reaches over and takes their hands)* Mom and Dad, you know me. You've known me all my life. You know I'm a good person. You know I love you and I'd never lie to you. Please, I know it's hard, but look into your hearts and think of all you know about me. I'm telling you the truth. An angel told me this baby would be the Son of God. He would grow up to be the King of Israel. This baby is a gift from God. Please, I want you to trust me.

(Long silence while Mother and Father stare at Mary.)

111

Angel: Trust in God. Trust in your daughter.

Father: *(Nods and looks at Mother)* She's always been a good girl.

Mother: *(Nods)* We do know you, *MARY*. If you say this baby is from God, then we believe you.

Father: We'll help you any way we can.

Mother: Does *JOSEPH* know?

Mary: I'm going to tell him next.

Scene Three: Mary And Joseph

Mary: *(Walks up steps) JOSEPH*, come in here. I've got something to tell you.

(Joseph walks in.)

Angel: *(Right behind Joseph — resting her hand on his back)* Trust *MARY*.

Mary: *(Sits down on chair opposite two chairs together)* I think you'd better sit down.

Joseph: *(Sits)* What is it, *MARY*?

Mary: I want you to listen to my whole story before you say anything. It's going to be a shock, but an angel came into my room and talked to me.

Joseph: An angel!

Angel: Trust in God, *JOSEPH*. Trust in *MARY*.

Mary: There's no easy way to say this. *(Hesitates)* The angel told me God has chosen me for a very special purpose. She said I am greatly blessed! I'm ... *(Hesitates)* I'm going to have a baby.

Joseph: *(Silent for a moment, then calmly)* Go on; I'm listening.

Angel: Trust.

Mary: *JOSEPH*, you know me. You've known me all my life. You know I'm a good person. You know I love you and I'd never lie to you. Please, I know it's hard, but look into your heart and think of all you know about me. I'm telling you the truth. An angel told me this baby would be the Son of God. He would grow up to be the King of Israel. This baby is a gift from God. Please, I want you to trust me.

112

Joseph: You can't honestly expect me to believe that!

Angel: *(Shakes Joseph's shoulder; says sternly)* I said trust.

Mary: It's true, *JOSEPH*!

Joseph: You must think I'm stupid.

Mary: No, I think you're a good man who loves God.

Joseph: I won't make a fuss about this. I won't tell anyone you're expecting a baby, but our engagement is off. *(Gets up)*

(Angel pulls back her hand to swat him. He moves and she misses, and Joseph walks out.)

Angel: *(Puts her hands on her hips, annoyed)* This isn't over, *JOSEPH*!

Youth 6:   Matthew 1:18-25

This is how the birth of Jesus Christ came about: His mother Mary was pledged to be married to Joseph, but before they came together she was found to be with child through the Holy Spirit. Because Joseph was a righteous man and did not want to expose her to public disgrace, he had in mind to divorce her quietly.

But after he had considered this, an angel of the Lord appeared to him in a dream and said, "Joseph, son of David, do not be afraid to take Mary home as your wife, because what is conceived in her is from the Holy Spirit. She will give birth to a son, and you are to give him the name Jesus, because he will save his people from their sins."

All this took place to fulfill what the Lord had said through the prophet: "The virgin will be with child and will give birth to a son and they will call him Immanuel" which means, God with us.

When Joseph woke up, he did what the angel of the Lord he had commanded him and took Mary home as his wife.

(Pauses for a moment; looks out at people) That's how it happened then. If it happened today ...

Scene Four: Angel And Joseph

(Joseph is sleeping on the stage. Three chairs are turned to be a bed for him to sleep on. Hold for laughter in this scene.)

Angel: *(Comes to him and circles a wand over his head and speaks politely) JOSEPH*, you should have trusted *MARY*.

(Joseph stirs but doesn't wake up.)

Angel: *(A little louder) JOSEPH*, I'm disappointed in you. *(Circles wand with hanging streamers so it tickles Joseph's face)*

113

(Joseph waves hand at streamers, stirs again, stays asleep.)

Angel: God's disappointed, too, **JOSEPH**. *(Taps Joseph on the head with wand)*

(Joseph rolls over.)

Angel: *(Very annoyed)* It's not good to disappoint God, **JOSEPH**. *(Whacks Joseph on the head with her wand)*

(Joseph yells in fear, falls out of bed, then jumps to his feet with his arms over his head. Hold for laughs.)

Angel: *(Sternly, points wand at Joseph)* The baby **MARY** will have is the Son of God. Marry her and name the baby Jesus, because he will save his people from their sins.

Joseph: Yes, all right! I'll do it! Don't hurt me!

Angel: *(Sweetly)* Did I forget to say "Fear not"?

(Joseph nods — big motions with his head — very afraid.)

Youth 7:   Luke 2:1-7

In those days Caesar Augustus issued a decree that a census should be taken of the entire Roman world. This was the first census that took place while Quirinius was governor of Syria. And everyone went to his own town to register.

So Joseph also went up from the town of Nazareth in Galilee to Judea, to Bethlehem the town of David, because he belonged to the house and line of David. He went there to register with Mary, who was pledged to be married to him and was expecting a child. While they were there, the time came for the baby to be born, and she gave birth to her firstborn, a son. She wrapped him in cloths and put him in a manger, because there was no room for them in the inn.

(Pauses for a moment; looks out at people) That's how it happened then. If it happened today ...

Scene Five: Innkeeper And Joseph

(Turn three folding chairs with back to congregation. Hang cardboard sign on chairs, saying, "[pick a local business] And Inn — No Vacancies." Innkeeper is dressed as a gardener because his business is a lawn service. If you pick a different local business, use appropriate costume.)

Joseph: We've looked everywhere, Mr. *(insert name of business owner)*. We need a room for the night. Can't you help us?

Innkeeper: Look around you; there are people sleeping on every inch of the floor. I even have people in the kitchen and in my own room. We are full.

114

Angel: *(Behind Innkeeper — hand on his shoulder)* Let them stay in the little shed behind the church where you store the lawn equipment.

Joseph: I think my wife is going to have a baby. Tonight. I have to find her shelter. We can't stay outside tonight.

Innkeeper: There is nothing for you here. Every person in town has family visiting because of the census. Every church in town has people lining the floor. Move along.

Angel: *(Shakes Innkeeper's shoulder)* Find a place for them.

Joseph: I've learned it's a bad idea to tell my wife, "No."

Innkeeper: Bad idea? What do you mean?

Angel: *(Lifts wand, waves dangles on Innkeepers head while shaking his shoulder)* There is room in the shed. Tell them they can stay there.

Joseph: *(Afraid of the angel who visited him)* My wife is just not a woman you want to upset. She's got powerful friends.

Innkeeper: Are you threatening me?

Joseph: No, I didn't mean it that way.

Innkeeper: *(Angrily)* We're full up.

Angel: Last chance. *(Whacks Innkeeper with wand)* Tell them you have room in the shed.

Innkeeper: *(Swats at place he got hit like it was a fly landing on him)* Get out of here!

(Joseph turns away sadly.)

Angel: That does it! *(Pulls out lightning bolt; pokes him with it)*

(Innkeeper jumps, yells, looks around, sees nothing — expect laughter here.)

Angel: The shed! *(Whacks him with the wand again)*

Innkeeper: Wait! There *is* a little shed out back you could stay in. It's dirty and small but it will at least be shelter.

Joseph: Why didn't you say so before?

Innkeeper: *(Shrugs)* It just hit me.

Youth 8: Luke 2:8-14

And there were shepherds living out in the fields nearby, keeping watch over their flocks at night. An angel of the Lord appeared to them, and the glory of the Lord shone around them, and they were terrified. But the angel said to them, "Do not be afraid. I bring you good news of great joy that will be for all the people. Today in the town of David a Savior has been born to you; he is Christ the Lord. This will be a sign to you: You will find a baby wrapped in cloths and lying in a manger."

Suddenly a great company of the heavenly host appeared with the angel, praising God and saying, "Glory to God in the highest, and on earth peace to men on whom his favor rests."

Song "While By Our Sheep" (arrangement © 1979,
(All children, Singspiration, found in *Praise! Our Songs And*
as indicated below) *Hymns,* Zondervan, Grand Rapids, Michigan)

1. **(all)** While by our sheep we watched that night, glad tidings brought an angel bright.
Chorus

(girls) How great our joy!	**(echo boys)** How great our joy!
Joy! Joy! Joy!	Joy! Joy! Joy!
Praise ye the Lord in heaven on high.	Praise ye the Lord in heaven on high.

2. **(all)** There shall be born so he did say, in Bethlehem today.
Chorus

(girls) How great our joy	**(echo boys)** How great our joy!
Joy! Joy! Joy!	Joy! Joy! Joy!
Praise ye the Lord in heaven on high.	Praise ye the Lord in heaven on high.

3. **(all)** There shall the child lie in a stall, this child who shall redeem us all.
Chorus

(girls) How great our joy!	**(echo boys)** How great our joy!
Joy! Joy! Joy!	Joy! Joy! Joy!
Praise ye the Lord in heaven on high.	Praise ye the Lord in heaven on high.

Youth 9: When the angels had left them and gone into heaven, the shepherds said to one another, "Let's go to Bethlehem and see this thing that has happened, which the Lord has told us about."

So they hurried off and found Mary and Joseph, and the baby, who was lying in the manger. When they had seen him, they spread the word concerning what had been told them about this child, and all who heard it were amazed at what the shepherds said to them. But Mary treasured up all these things and pondered them in her heart. The shepherds returned, glorifying and praising God for all the things they had heard and seen, which were just as they had been told.

(Pauses for a moment; looks out at people) That's how it happened then. If it happened today ...

Scene Six: Shepherd, Wife, And Son

(Shepherds have cardboard sheep suspended from their belt loops.)

Shepherd: *(Makes call on cell phone)* Hi, *(insert name of wife of local farmer, carpenter, outdoor worker, etc.).*

Wife: *(On her cell phone)* Hi, *(insert name of local farmer, carpenter, outdoor worker, etc.)*.

Shepherd: I think I'm going to be late. Something weird just happened.

Wife: What?

Shepherd: *(Hesitantly)* Well, *(insert name of child cast as shepherd's son)* and I were checking the sheep and an angel came and talked to us.

Wife: *(Amazed)* An angel?

Shepherd: She came right down out of heaven and told me I should go into *(insert the name of your town)* and look in that little shed behind the Presbyterian Church *(your own church or some other building in town)*. She said there was a woman in there who had just had a baby.

Wife: A baby, in that rickety little shed?

Shepherd: *(To son)* She doesn't believe me.

Son: *(Takes the phone away from his father)* That's what the angel said, Mom. We both heard it.

Wife: *(Sympathetically)* *(insert name of son)*, sometimes a person can inhale those fumes from the sprayer *(or those fumes from the car, those fumes from the lawn fertilizer)* and get a little confused.

Son: *(Pulls phone away from ear)* Dad, Mom thinks we're loopy on pesticide *(gas fumes, and so on)*.

Shepherd: *(Takes the phone back)* I didn't imagine this! The angel told me to follow the star and I can see the star right now *(Points at ceiling of church)* shining brightly in the sky. The angel told me the baby in that shed would save our whole nation.

Wife: How can a baby do that?

Shepherd: I don't know, but the next thing I knew the whole sky was full of angels praising God. I'm going to check that shed. I have to.

Wife: All right, if you have to, then you have to. How long will you be gone?

Shepherd: I'm just guessing ... *(Pauses and thinks)*; give me four hours.

Wife: Four hours! Your dinner's going to be ruined!

Shepherd: You didn't see this angel, *(insert name of farmer's wife)*.

Wife: Okay. Yes, I agree you have to go. But, *(insert name of farmer)*?

Shepherd: Yes, *(insert name of farmer's wife)*?

Wife: *(Pauses a while)* We don't have any sheep. *(Hold for laughter)*

Shepherd: Gotta go! *(Hangs up phone)*

(Wife hangs up phone — looks out at the congregation for a few seconds — shrugs.)

Shepherd: *(To son) (insert name of child)*, where'd you get these sheep? *(Laughter — wait or last line is lost)*

Son: I thought they were yours. *(Laughter)*

Youth 10:   Matthew 2:1-2, 9b-12
    After Jesus was born in Bethlehem in Judea, during the time of King Herod, Magi from the east came to Jerusalem and asked, "Where is the one who has been born King of the Jews? We saw his star in the east and have come to worship him."
    And the star they had seen in the east went ahead of them until it stopped over the place where the child was. When they saw the star, they were overjoyed. On coming to the house, they saw the child with his mother Mary and they bowed down and worshiped him. Then they opened their treasures and presented him with gifts of gold and of incense and of myrrh. And having been warned in a dream not to go back to Herod, they returned to their country by another route.
    (Pauses a moment; looks out at people.) That's how it happened then. If it happened today ...

Scene Seven: Wise Man And Wife

Wise Man: *(With cardboard tractor costume; cell phone) (insert name of local woman)*?

Wife: *(On phone)* Hi, *(insert name of woman's husband)*. Are you headed home?

Wise Man: I think I'm going to be late. Something weird just happened.

Wife: What?

Wise Man: You know how I like to watch the stars when I'm out spraying fertilizer late at night?

Wife: Yes.

Wise Man: All of a sudden one of the stars was bigger than all the rest. It grew and it started shining all the way down to the ground. And, I know this is hard to believe, but God told me I have to go to the place that star is shining. He said there is a baby born in that place that is the Messiah. The Son of God. I have to go there and see this baby and worship him.

118

Wife: *(insert name of husband)*, sometimes a person can inhale those chemical fumes from the sprayer and get a little confused.

Wise Man: I didn't imagine this! I've got to follow that star!

Wife: All right, if you have to, then you have to. Where are you going?

Wise Man: Wherever the star leads. I won't know where I'm going until I get there.

Wife: How long will you be gone?

Wise Man: I'm just guessing ... *(Pauses and thinks);* give me four years.

Wife: Four years! We just had a grandchild! We've got a wedding this summer! *(In this family they did just have a grandchild and a wedding — personalize the script)* Four years!

Wise Man: Gotta go!

Wife: Wait! *(Long pause)* I'll miss you.

Wise Man: I'll miss you, too, but I have to go.

Wife: Can I come, too?

Wise Man: Sure, I'll be home in ten minutes. *(Hangs up)*

(Wife hangs up phone — looks out at congregation for a few seconds — shrugs.)

Youth 11: Two thousand years ago the Wise Men started their long journey. They would be away from home for years. The shepherds abandoned the sheep that were their only way to make a living. Angels appeared in someone's home ... then in a dream ... then in the night sky, and opened the hearts of many to make them accept something that no one would have accepted under normal circumstances. One miracle after another prepared these people for the truth — the Son of God was coming to live among them. The people the angels visited were simple faithful believers, like we are. And if we would see that light in the sky and hear the angels' voices, we would do just as they did so long ago ... *(Pauses for dramatic effect)* ... if it happened today.

Youth 12: *(Gives closing prayer)* Please join me in prayer.
    Dear Lord, thank you for your son Jesus. Help us spread the word. Thank you for letting us be part of the wide circle of believers. Thank you for Christmas. Thank you for this chance to celebrate the day that Jesus was sent into the world. Amen.

Youth 13: *(Gives benediction and announces boys' song)* Jesus is the way, the Truth, and the Life. He is the only path to God's love. Jesus is the cornerstone of our faith. Jesus is the source of our love for each other. Two thousand years ago, or right now, God is the same. While we are separated one from another, let's stay close in our hearts, bound together by the joy Jesus brought to the world.

Song "Joy To The World"
(Older boys sing)
1. **(all)** Joy to the world, the Lord is come.
Let earth receive her King.
Let every heart prepare him room,
(duet) And heaven and nature sing,
(quartet) And heaven and nature sing,
(all) And heaven and heaven and nature sing.

2. **(all)** Joy to the world, the Savior reigns.
Let men their songs employ.
While fields and floods, Rocks, hills, and plains,
(duet) Repeat the sounding joy,
(quartet) Repeat the sounding joy,
(all) Repeat, repeat the sounding joy.

3. **(all)** He rules the world with truth and grace.
And makes the nations prove.
The glories of his righteousness,
(duet) And wonders of his love,
(quartet) And wonders of his love,
(all) And wonders, and wonders of his love.

Youth 14: As you enjoy the fun of Christmas, the gifts, the food, the reunions, may the peace of God be with you all until we meet again. May you know the love and joy that come from accepting the baby born on that long ago night as the Savior of the modern world. May your Christmas spirit truly be a holy one. And, remember, if an angel could come to those people then ... it could happen to any of us, today. Keep your heart open to the continuing miracle of Christmas. Please join in singing verses 1 and 2 of "The First Noel."

(Children begin exiting immediately. Don't wait for end of first verse.)

(Young person plays a piano or instrumental postlude.)

Do You Hear What I Hear?

A Sunday School
Christmas Program

Cynthia E. Cowen

Contents

Sunday School Christmas Program
Do You Hear What I Hear?
(Name of Church)
(Date and Time)

Prelude

Fifth Graders "Jingle Bells"

Scene 1: Mr. Greedy's Department Store

Scene 2: Nazareth

Third Graders "It Came Upon A Midnight Clear"

Fourth Graders "O Come, All Ye Faithful"

Third and Fourth Graders "O Little Town Of Bethlehem"

Congregation "O Little Town Of Bethlehem"
For Christ is born of Mary, and gathered all above
While mortals sleep, the angels keep
their watch of wondering love.
O morning stars together, proclaim the holy birth,
And praises sing to God the king and peace to all the earth!

How silently, how silently the wondrous gift is giv'n!
So God imparts to human hearts the blessings of his heav'n.
No ear may hear his coming; but, in this world of sin,
Where meek souls will receive him,
still the dear Christ enters in.

Scene 3: Bethlehem Inn

Second Graders "Angels We Have Heard On High"

Scene 4: Bethlehem Stable

Second Graders "Angels We Have Heard On High"

Congregation   "Oh, Come, Little Children"

    Oh, come, little children, oh, come, one and all,
    To Bethlehem haste to the manger so small.
    God's Son for a gift has been sent you this night
    To be your Redeemer, your Joy and Delight.
    See Mary and Joseph, with love-beaming eyes,
    Are gazing upon the rude bed where he lies,
    The shepherds are kneeling, with hearts full of love,
    While angels sing loud alleluias above.

First Graders, Preschool, and Kindergartners   "Joy To The World!"

First Graders, Preschool, and Kindergartners   "The First Noel"

Congregation   "We Three Kings"

    We three kings of Orient are,
    Bearing gifts we traverse afar
    Field and fountain, moor and mountain,
    Following yonder star.

    O star of wonder, star of night.
    Star with royal beauty bright,
    Westward leading, still proceeding.
    Guide us to thy perfect light.

    Glorious now behold him arise,
    King and God and Sacrifice;
    Alleluia, alleluia!
    Earth to heaven replies.

    O star of wonder, star of night.
    Star with royal beauty bright,
    Westward leading, still proceeding.
    Guide us to thy perfect light.

Youth and Congregation   "Away In A Manger"

    Away in a manger, no crib for a bed,
    The little Lord Jesus lay down his sweet head,
    The stars in the sky looked down where he lay,
    The little Lord Jesus asleep in the hay.

    The cattle are lowing, the poor baby wakes,
    But little Lord Jesus no crying he makes.
    I love thee, Lord Jesus, look down from the sky.
    And stay by my cradle 'til morning is nigh.

Be near me, Lord Jesus, I ask thee to stay
Close by me forever, and love me, I pray.
Bless all the dear children in thy tender care.
And fit us for heaven to live with thee there.

Sunday School Superintendent

All Youth   "Do You Hear What I Hear?"

Sunday School Superintendent

Congregation   "Hark! The Herald Angels Sing"
Hark! the herald angels sing,
"Glory to the newborn King;
Peace on earth, and mercy mild,
God and sinners reconciled."
Joyful all ye nations, rise,
Join the triumph of the skies;
With th' angelic host proclaim,
"Christ is born in Bethlehem."
Hark, the herald angels sing,
"Glory to the newborn King."

*Join us for cookies and beverage.

Do You Hear What I Hear?

(Program And Script)

Prelude

(Fifth Graders dressed in hats and scarves and ringing bells enter from side, singing "Jingle Bells.")

"Jingle Bells"
Dashing through the snow, in a one-horse open sleigh
O'er the fields we go, laughing all the way. Ha, ha, ha!
Bells on bob-tail ring, making spirits bright,
What fun it is to ride and sing a sleighing song tonight.

Jingle bells, jingle bells, jingle all the way,
Oh, what fun it is to ride in a one-horse open sleigh.
Jingle bells, jingle bells, jingle all the way,
Oh, what fun it is to ride in a one-horse open sleigh.

Youth 1: Are you ready for some Christmas fun tonight?

Youth 2: I'm set. But listen.

Youth 3: What's that you *hear*?

Youth 2: I don't know, but I distinctly *hear* something out of the ordinary.

Youth 1: Well, I *hear* sleigh bells.

(Youth in choir rings sleigh bells.)

Youth 3: Me, too. The horses are ready to go, so let's set off on our journey.

Youth 2: But I *hear* something more. There's just more to this night than a sleigh ride.

Youth 1: Well, Christmas is a time for fun! For sleigh rides and presents and songs.

Youth 2: But I'm serious. I *hear* something more.

Youth 3: You mean like there's more to this night than a good time?

Youth 2: I think so, but let's dash out of here and see what this night holds.

(Group leaves singing "Jingle Bells." Leaves three teachers dressed as clerks behind who stay in front and three narrators who move to the side.)

> Jingle bells, jingle bells, jingle all the way,
> Oh, what fun it is to ride in a one-horse open sleigh,
> Jingle bells, jingle bells, jingle all the way,
> Oh, what fun it is to ride in a one-horse open sleigh.

(Sign — "Mr. Greedy's Department Store." Clerks wear red, green, or Christmas aprons and hats. One carries a money bag.)

Clerk 1: Ding, ding. Ding, ding. Just *listen* to those cash registers go ding, ding.

Clerk 2: That's what Christmas is about, isn't it? *(Sings)* Do you *hear* what I *hear*?

Clerk 1: Yes, I *hear* the sound of money in our pockets. Christmas is a great season to make money. *(Jingles money bag.)*

Clerk 3: But I *hear* something more. Can't you *hear* it calling out there?

Clerk 1: *(Feels forehead of other clerk)* Are you well? Maybe you've got some seasonal bug.

Clerk 3: No, I think you two have a seasonal bug called "greed." I think there's more to this season than spending, spending, and spending. I just *hear* something more.

Clerk 2: Sure, there's more. It's getting, getting, getting!

Clerk 3: I think you're listening to the wrong Christmas spirit.

Clerk 1: So what is it you want us to *hear* this Christmas season?

Clerk 3: I bet we can *hear* a different message if we travel back in time to when it all began. Are you game?

Clerk 1: Why not?

Clerk 2: Let's go!

Clerk 3: And Church, listen to the voice of Christmas as it calls to you this night.

(Clerks and Sign Board leave.)

Traveling Music   "Do You Hear What I Hear?"

(Sign — "Nazareth." Joseph enters from side and lays down pretending to sleep.)

128

Narrator 1: Long ago in the city of Nazareth a miracle was about to occur.

(Angel enters from back door and approaches the sleeping Joseph. Touches him. Joseph rises.)

Narrator 2: Mary and Joseph were engaged to be married when Mary discovered she was pregnant. Then an angel of the Lord appeared to Joseph one night and told him:

Angel: Joseph, son of David, don't be afraid to take Mary as your wife because the baby in her is from the Holy Spirit. She will give birth to a son, and you will name him Jesus, because he will save his people from sin.

(Angel leaves. Mary enters from the side and Joseph goes to her.)

Joseph: Mary, come and *hear* what I have just heard. *(Whispers in her ear)*

Mary: Praise God, Joseph! You have *heard* what I *heard*. Blessed is the Lord who will bring us salvation. But listen, I *hear* the voices of young children coming to share our joy this night.

Traveling Music   "Do You Hear What I Hear?"

(Third Graders dressed as angels enter to traveling music. They take their place to sing.)

"It Came Upon A Midnight Clear"
    It came upon the midnight clear,
    That glorious song of old,
    From angels bending near the earth
    To touch their harps of gold:
    "Peace on the earth, good will to men,
    From heaven's all-gracious King!"
    The world in solemn stillness lay
    To hear the angels sing.

    Still through the cloven skies they come
    With peaceful wings unfurled;
    And still their heavenly music floats
    O'er all the weary world
    Above its sad and lowly plains
    They bend on hovering wing,
    And ever over its Babel sounds
    The blessed angels sing.

Narrator 3: At this same time Caesar gave an order to all the people that they must register in their hometowns. Joseph was from Bethlehem and so he and Mary set out for the city.

(Mary and Joseph move behind or around the group and walk out in front of them pretending to be traveling, then exit.)

Traveling Music   "Do You Hear What I Hear?"

(Fourth Graders dressed as angels enter to traveling music. They walk up the middle to stand in front to sing "O Come, All Ye Faithful.")

"O Come, All Ye Faithful"
 O come, all ye faithful, joyful and triumphant,
 O come ye, o come ye to Bethlehem!
 Come and behold him, born the King of angels!
 O come, let us adore him,
 O come, let us adore him,
 O come, let us adore him, Christ the Lord!

 Sing, choirs of angels, sing in exultation!
 Sing all ye citizens of heaven above!
 Glory to God, all glory in the highest!
 O come, let us adore him,
 O come, let us adore him,
 O come, let us adore him, Christ the Lord!

Narrator 2: Let us go to Bethlehem now.

(Fourth Grade and Third Grade sing verse 1 of "O Little Town of Bethlehem.")

"O Little Town of Bethlehem"
 O little town of Bethlehem, how still we see thee lie!
 Above thy deep and dreamless sleep the silent stars go by;
 Yet in thy dark streets shineth the everlasting light.
 The hopes and fears of all the years are met in thee tonight.

Narrator 2: Congregation, join us in singing the rest of this carol as our youth depart.

(Congregation joins in verses 2 and 3 as Fourth and Third Grades leave.)

Congregation
 For Christ is born of Mary, and gathered all above
 While mortals sleep, the angels keep
 their watch of wondering love.
 O morning stars together, proclaim the holy birth,
 And praises sing to God the king and peace to all the earth!

How silently, how silently the wondrous gift is giv'n!
So God imparts to human hearts the blessings of his heav'n.
No ear may hear his coming; but, in this world of sin,
Where meek souls will receive him still
The dear Christ enters in.

(While the congregation is singing, Mary and Joseph enter again. Three innkeepers enter and take their places in front. Sign — "Bethlehem.")

Narrator 1: No ear may *hear* his coming ...

Narrator 2: But in this world of sin ...

Narrator 3: Where meek souls will receive him still, the dear Christ enters in.

Narrator 1: Let us pray. Lord Jesus, we come to you with ears *hearing* the story of your birth. Help us to respond to your voice calling us to come to you. We open our hearts to receive you anew. Come into our hearts, Lord Jesus. In your precious name we pray. Amen.

Narrator 2: But back to our story. After walking for some time, Mary and Joseph arrived in Bethlehem and began to search for a place to spend the night.

Traveling Music   "Do You Hear What I Hear?"

(Joseph walks to first innkeeper. Motions to Mary, but the first innkeeper just shakes his head "no" at Joseph's request and walks off stage. Joseph and Mary move to the second who throws up hands, shakes head, and leaves. Couple hang heads, then move to the pulpit to take place for dialogue with third innkeeper who has moved to the lectern. While this is happening, Second Graders dressed as angels enter from the back of the church to traveling music. Youth enters with sign — "Stable." Another carries a manger and puts it down. Second Graders take their place and sing "Angels We Have Heard On High.")

"Angels We Have Heard On High"
    Angels we have heard on high,
    Sweetly singing o'er the plains;
    And the mountains in reply
    Echoing their joyous strains.
    Gloria in excelsis Deo.
    Gloria in excelsis Deo.

    Shepherds, why this jubilee?
    Why your joyous songs prolong?
    What the gladsome tidings be
    Which inspire your heavenly song?
    Gloria in excelsis Deo.
    Gloria in excelsis Deo.

Joseph: Sir, please help us. We've traveled a long way, and we need a room.

Innkeeper: I am sorry, but I have no rooms. It's census time, and the city is bursting with all the people coming to be counted by the Roman government.

Joseph: Please sir, my wife is pregnant, and there is no place for us to stay. Hear our cries for help.

Innkeeper: *(Scratches the side of his face and sighs)* Well, if you would like, you could spend the night in my stable. *(Points to stable)*

Joseph: That will work just fine. Thank you!

(Second Grade sings final verse of "Angels We Have Heard On High.")

> Come to Bethlehem, and see
> Him whose birth the angels sing;
> Come adore on bended knee,
> Christ the Lord, our newborn King.
> Gloria in excelsis Deo.
> Gloria in excelsis Deo.

(Second Graders return to seats while pianist continues to play "Angels We Have Heard On High." Mary and Joseph go to the stable and sit. Manger is brought out.)

Mary: UOOOH! *(Hugs middle as in labor)* Joseph, I think that it's time for the baby to be born! Let's have the congregation join us in a song of celebration, "Oh, Come, Little Children."

Congregation   "Oh, Come, Little Children"

> Oh, come, little children, oh, come, one and all,
> To Bethlehem haste to the manger so small.
> God's Son for a gift has been sent you this night
> To be your Redeemer, your Joy and Delight.
>
> See Mary and Joseph, with love-beaming eyes,
> Are gazing upon the rude bed where he lies,
> The shepherds are kneeling, with hearts full of love,
> While angels sing loud alleluias above.

(Mary and Joseph go off stage. Pianist changes traveling music as Preschool and Kindergarten children, dressed in lamb ears or other animal headbands, enter with First Graders with gold garland around heads. Youth gather together in front to sing.)

Narrator 2: What joy young children bring. Hear them as they sing!

(Groups sing "Joy To The World!")

"Joy To The World!"
    Joy to the world, the Lord is come!
    Let earth receive its King.
    Let every heart, prepare him room.

    And heav'n and nature sing,
    And heav'n and nature sing,
    And heav'n and nature sing.

    He rules the earth with truth and love,
    And makes the nations see
    The glories of his righteousness,

    And wonders of his love,
    And wonders of his love,
    And wonders of his love.

Narrator 2: What joy came into our world that night. The earth praised God as the light of the world entered our darkness.

(First Graders and Preschool and Kindergartners sing "The First Noel.")

"The First Noel"
    The first Noel the angel did say
    Was to certain poor shepherds in fields as they lay;
    In fields where they lay keeping their sheep,
    On a cold winter's night that was so deep.

    Noel, Noel, Noel, Noel,
    Born is the King of Israel.

    And by the light of that same star,
    Three wise men came from country far;
    To seek for a King was their intent,
    And to follow the star wherever it went.

(Star appears held up high or light up above youth.)

    Noel, Noel, Noel, Noel,
    Born is the King of Israel.

Narrator 1: Church, are you hearing the message of Christmas? Let us rejoice in the youth who have shared this message with us. Join us in singing "We Three Kings."

133

(Youth exit. Youth with star stays. Congregation sings verses 1 and 4 of "We Three Kings." Mary and Joseph go down in front with manger. Three Wise Men enter from side with their gifts. Take place in back of Mary and Joseph.)

Congregation   "We Three Kings"

We three kings of Orient are,
Bearing gifts we traverse afar
Field and fountain, moor and mountain,
Following yonder star.

O star of wonder, star of night.
Star with royal beauty bright,
Westward leading, still proceeding.
Guide us to thy perfect light.

Glorious now behold him arise,
King and God and Sacrifice;
Alleluia, alleluia!
Earth to heaven replies.

O star of wonder, star of night.
Star with royal beauty bright,
Westward leading, still proceeding.
Guide us to thy perfect light.

Narrator 3: At the same time three Wise Men were traveling through the desert when they saw a star high in the eastern sky.

Wise Man 1: Look! It's the star of the King! *(Points to star)*

Wise Man 2: Come on; let's follow it!

Narrator 1: Mary had given birth to our Savior, Jesus Christ. She wrapped him in bands of cloth and placed him in a manger.

(Mary places baby Jesus in the manger. Joseph stands next to her.)

Wise Man 3: We have brought gifts of gold *(Pauses as Wise Man 1 kneels and hands to Mary)*, frankincense *(Pauses as Wise Man 2 kneels and hands to Mary)*, and myrrh for the child born a king *(Kneels and gives to Mary)*.

Narrator 2: Yes, Jesus is the one born King of kings. Hear the Word of the Lord concerning his reign.

Narrator 3: "A child has been born to us; God has given a son to us. He will be responsible for leading the people. His name will be Wonderful Counselor, Powerful God, Father Who Lives Forever, Prince of Peace. Power and peace will be in his kingdom and will continue to grow forever. He will rule as king on David's throne and over David's kingdom. He will make it strong by ruling with justice and goodness from now on and forever. The Lord All-Powerful will do this because of his strong love for his people." A reading from the prophet Isaiah, chapter 9, verses 6-7 (*New Century Version*).

Sunday School Superintendent: I wish to thank all our youth who made this a night filled with hearing God's story of his great love for all of us. So let's welcome all our youth back as they come to share in our final number. Let's sing "Away In A Manger."

(All youth enter and take their place as congregation sings "Away In A Manger." Oldest youth first, fill in as groups with youngest ones in front. Mary and Joseph and Wise Men stay in front.)

"Away In A Manger"
    Away in a manger, no crib for a bed,
    The little Lord Jesus lay down his sweet head,
    The stars in the sky looked down where he lay,
    The little Lord Jesus asleep in the hay.

    The cattle are lowing, the poor baby wakes,
    But little Lord Jesus no crying he makes.
    I love thee, Lord Jesus, look down from the sky.
    And stay by my cradle 'til morning is nigh.

    Be near me, Lord Jesus, I ask thee to stay
    Close by me forever, and love me, I pray.
    Bless all the dear children in thy tender care.
    And fit us for heaven to live with thee there.

Sunday School Superintendent: Do you *hear* what our youth have told you of this Christmas? The joy that floods our hearts is not one that comes from sleigh rides, or purchasing gifts, or getting gifts. It is receiving the Lord Jesus Christ into our hearts. Do you *hear* what I *hear*, Church? Listen as our youth share their final song, "Do You Hear What I Hear?"

Youth   "Do You Hear What I Hear?"
    (Copyright words and music by Noel Regney and Gloria Shayne; Hal Leonard, publisher)

Sunday School Superintendent: Did you *hear* what we *heard*? We pray you did. Go in the name of the Child of Bethlehem who loves you and has come to bring you salvation. Join us for cookies and beverage. Now let's all sing "Hark! The Herald Angels Sing."

Traveling Music   "Hark! The Herald Angels Sing"

(Sung by youth and congregation)
    Hark! the herald angels sing,
    "Glory to the newborn King;
    Peace on earth, and mercy mild,
    God and sinners reconciled."
    Joyful all ye nations, rise,
    Join the triumph of the skies;
    With th' angelic host proclaim,
    "Christ is born in Bethlehem."
    Hark, the herald angels sing,
    "Glory to the newborn King."

Traveling Music   "Hark! The Herald Angels Sing"

Leader's Helps

Fifth Grade
- Song: "Jingle Bells"
- Dressed in hats with scarves
- Carry sleigh bells to ring

Third Grade
- Song: "It Came Upon A Midnight Clear"
- Song: "O Little Town of Bethlehem," verse 1
- Dressed as angels or in nice outfits with gold garland around heads

Fourth Grade
- Song: "O, Come All Ye Faithful"
- Song: "O Little Town of Bethlehem," verse 1
- Dressed as angels or in nice outfits with gold garland around heads

Second Grade
- Song: "Angels We Have Heard On High"
- Dressed as angels or in nice outfits with gold garland around heads

Preschool and Kindergarten
- Song: "Joy To The World"
- Song: Refrain of "The First Noel"
- Dressed as animals (headbands with ears such as sheep; may blacken noses)

First Grade
- Song: "Joy To The World"
- Song: "The First Noel," verses 1 and 2
- Dressed as shepherds

All groups
- "Do You Hear What I Hear?"

Participants
- Use youth musicians and teachers or other special music in prelude
- Pianist
- Sunday School Superintendent
- Youth 1, 2, and 3

- Clerks 1, 2, and 3
  - Can be teachers
  - Wear green, red, or Christmas aprons
  - One carries money and money bag
  - Money bag
- Narrators 1, 2, and 3
- Angel
- Joseph
- Mary
- 3 Innkeepers (two don't speak)
- 3 Wise Men (carry three gifts)

Other Props

Signs
  - Mr. Greedy's Department Store
  - Nazareth
  - Bethlehem
  - Stable

Manger

Bench for Mary and Joseph

Star

May use a star and a stable backdrop

Congregational Songs:
- "O Little Town Of Bethlehem," verses 2 and 3
- "Oh, Come, Little Children," verses 1 and 3
- "We Three Kings Of Orient Are," verses 1 and 5
- "Away In A Manger"
- "Hark! The Herald Angels Sing," verse 1

"Do You Hear What I Hear?"

Secure sheet music for tune and permission to copy from copyright holder. Copyright words and music by Noel Regney and Gloria Shayne (Hal Leonard, publisher). Obtain music for your use.

Christmas Wonder

Children's Sermons
For Advent And Christmas

Elaine M. Ward

Contents

Introduction

Christmas is the sounds and smells, tastes and touches, sights and stories shared with children around the altar, that "manger" where stories are born and stored.

Christmas is the expression of love given and received, God's love for us and our love for God and one another. Advent is the preparation for that giving and receiving.

For me, Christmas is the wonder seen on children's faces as they hear stories of God's grace and love, Jesus' compassion, and the gifts of the Holy Spirit.

Let Christmas Begin
Tuck the child in,
Tuck the child in,
Jesus is born,
Let Christmas begin.

No cradle, just a manger
Where cows and sheep are fed,
No blanket, just the hay there,
No pillow for his head,
No robe, nor shawl, nor sleepers,
Just swaddling cloths to wear.
No hospital, nor warm home,
But love and care are there,
And angels for his choir,
And shepherds for his friends,
And kings who come to worship,
As their long journey ends.

Away from the crowds,
Away from the din,
Jesus is born!
Let Christmas begin!

First Sunday Of Advent
New Friends

Psalm 25:1-10

John was six when he moved to the new city, the new house, the new school. Because everything was new, his one wish was to make a new friend.

The first day of school John met Bill. When he saw him, he said, "Hi." But Bill did not reply.

John put his hand in his pocket and asked, "Want some gum?" It was recess and the class was on the playground, the only place gum was allowed.

Bill ignored John, turned his back, and walked away.

John ignored the empty feeling inside himself and followed Bill. "I heard a great joke ..."

"Beat it!" Bill said, staring hard at John.

The sky darkened. The rest of the day John had trouble concentrating on his school work.

When John returned home that afternoon, Mother asked, "How was your first day at school?" John did not reply, but the look on his face showed that he was not happy.

Mother poured a glass of milk and put a plate of cookies before John, as she said, "It takes time to make friends."

John was about to complain when crunching his cookie, he heard, "Bzzz. Bzzz. Bzzz."

"I'll get it," he cried, running to answer the doorbell. Mother followed.

Bill, his brother Andrew, who was seven, and his brother James, who was nine, stood at the door.

James spoke for his brothers. "Bill wants to fight John."

Mother asked, "Does Bill know how to fight?"

All three boys shouted, "Sure!" Andrew and James added, "We taught him."

There was silence. John did not want to fight. He only wanted a new friend.

Mother said, "I am sorry but John does not know how to fight. Could you come back tomorrow instead?"

As long as they could fight, to show how strong they were, they agreed. The next day they returned as they had promised. Bill had a scratch across his face. James had a band-aid on his arm, and Andrew had a black eye.

"Bzzz. Bzzz. Bzzz." Mother and John answered the door. Mother exclaimed, "Oh, you have come back to fight. I wonder, however, if you would like to taste some of the cookies I just baked?"

Smiles appeared on sour faces. "Sure!" they said, coming inside the house together, and with milk and cookies inside his stomach, James said, "John, you wanta play 'King of the mountain'?"

Talk together: Why do you think Bill wanted to fight John? Have you ever met a bully, someone who wanted to fight? How did peace happen? Which was the better idea, to fight or to be friends? Which of the boys lived by the words of the psalmist, "In you, God, I trust"?

Prayer: Dear God, where there is a bully, let there be love. Where there is fighting, let there be peace. Where there is fear, let there be trust in your steadfast love and presence. Amen.

Second Sunday Of Advent
Pastor John

Luke 1:68-79

Last week we heard of a boy named John who trusted God and wanted peace rather than fighting.

Once there was a man named John, who lived in the desert, the wilderness, preaching and baptizing in the River Jordan. This John wore the skins of wild animals. His hair was long and never cut. He ate honey and locusts, a beetle-like insect. The honey stuck to his black beard and he smelled like the animal skin he wore.

John was a "called" man, a man called by God to prepare the people for the coming of Jesus. John preached passionately to the people, "Prepare ye the way of the Lord." He was called John the Baptist.

Years and years and years later, it might be today, there was a preacher named John. The people called him "Pastor John."

When it was time for Pastor John to preach his sermon, he stood up and climbed into the pulpit. He began to preach passionately, as John the Baptist did. The papers on the pulpit flew to the floor as he threw out his arms. His glasses fell off his nose and spittle ran out of his mouth, as he shook his finger and shouted.

One of the children, sitting in a pew below the pulpit, reached for his mother's hand and whispered, "Mommy, I'm afraid of that man in the box. What if they let him out?"

Then suddenly Pastor John was quiet. There was silence in the sanctuary, as he read from the Bible:

"When John the Baptist's father, Zechariah, was filled with the Holy Spirit, he spoke, 'By the tender mercy of our God, the dawn from on high will break upon us, to give light to those who sit in darkness and in the shadow of death, to guide our feet into the way of peace.'"

The child let go of his mother's hand, took a deep breath, and smiled peacefully.

Talk together: What do you know about John the Baptist? Why did Pastor John get so excited? Why was the child afraid?

Prayer: Let us pray the words of Zechariah together. "By the tender mercy of our God, the dawn from on high will break upon us, to give light to those who sit in darkness and in the shadow of death, to guide our feet into the way of peace." Amen.

Third Sunday Of Advent
The Right Mary

Isaiah 12:2-6

"Hail, Mary!" the angel cried.

"No time now," Mary replied, grabbing her broom.

"Favored one of God ..." the angel tried again.

"I'll bet you say that to all the maidens, to all the girls."

"The Lord is with you!" The angel was persistent.

"Yes, I know, but will he help me find my water jug? If I don't hurry, I'll be last in line at the well to get water."

Once more the angel tried, "Do not be afraid, Mary. You have found favor with God ..."

"Of course. Thanks, and I really would like to spend more time chatting with you, but ..."

A flurry of wings filled the room.

Then silence.

It was the wrong Mary ...

For when the angel Gabriel came to Mary, the mother of Jesus, to tell her that she would be the mother of Jesus, Mary (the right Mary) sang with joy. Mary trusted and was not afraid; as the prophet said, "For the Lord God is my strength and my might. Sing praise to the Lord, sing for joy."

Talk together: How did the angel know this was the wrong Mary?

Prayer: Dear God, hear our songs of joy and praise as we thank you for all our blessings. Amen.

Fourth Sunday Of Advent
Best Blessing

Luke 1:39-45

When Mary went to visit her relative Elizabeth, the child in Elizabeth's womb leaped, and Elizabeth was filled with the Holy Spirit and said, with a loud cry, "Mary, *blessed* are you among women and blessed is the life of the child in your womb."

Sarah was loved. Her mother read stories to her at night and prepared her favorite meals. Her father played table games with her as they laughed together at his jokes. Her brother drew pictures with her that they hung on the refrigerator door.

One Sunday after church Sarah asked, "What is a 'be-at-a-tude'?" Her mother explained, "It's a blessing, a special gift from God." Her brother added, "It's like a hot fudge sundae, Sarah." Her father laughed and said, "Well, perhaps, for Sarah."

Each night before she went to sleep Sarah thought of one blessing she had had that day. There was running with her dog Rascal, her teacher smiling at her, the yellow daffodils blooming in the backyard, but best of all was her birthday that was about to be.

Sarah crossed off each day on her calendar. Only six more days. Five, four, three, two, one ... Then the next morning her father said, "Happy birthday, Sarah." Her mother said, "Happy birthday, Sarah." Her brother said, "Happy birthday, Sarah." Sarah climbed into her mother's lap and asked, "Do you know what my best blessing is?" Without waiting for her mother's reply, she said, "My best *blessing* is being born!"

Talk together: What is your best blessing?

Prayer: Thank you, God, for the great blessing of life. Help us live it abundantly, with wonder and joy. Amen.

Christmas Eve
Go With Haste

Luke 2:1-20

Read aloud the Nativity story in Luke.

It was Christmas Eve on the farm. Bill had just finished helping his father put the cows and horses and sheep in the barn for the night. Bill and his father closed the barn door and stepped out into the dark. It was very cold and windy. The lashing wind whipped the snow across Bill's face as they struggled into the house.

Inside, the kitchen was warm. Bill smelled the stew cooking on the stove, as Father said, "I don't know if we will be able to get to church tonight because of the snow."

Mother looked up from the stove where she was stirring the stew. "It would not seem like Christmas if we could not attend church on Christmas Eve."

Beth, Bill's sister, stopped pouring milk. "Father, I'm in the Christmas choir," she said. "I have to be there."

Father replied, "Let's have dinner and then we will see."

Bill listened to the howling wind all through dinner. At last he put down his fork and asked, "Was it hard for the shepherds to get to Bethlehem that first Christmas?"

No one replied. At last Mother said, "Why don't you get the Bible, Bill, and we will read."

Bill brought the Bible to the table and read, "When the angels went away from them into heaven, the shepherds said to one another, 'Let us go to Bethlehem and see this thing that has happened, which the Lord has made known to us.' And they went with haste, and found Mary and Joseph, and the babe lying in the manger."

It was quiet around the table when Bill finished reading. Bill got up from the table to look out at the cold, dark, windy night. Father pushed back his chair and joined Bill at the window. "The car is warm and it is not that far," he said, as if thinking aloud. "Yes, let us go with haste."

When Bill and his family arrived at church, they sang with great joy, as the angels had on that first Christmas Eve long ago, and when the minister read, "And they went with haste," from the Christmas story in the Bible, Bill and his family smiled at one another, for they had experienced that part of the story.

Talk together: Why do you think the shepherds "went with haste"? Why did they hurry? Where do you go "with haste"?

Beth sang "Silent Night" in the choir that Christmas Eve. We can sing "Silent Night," as well. (Invite the congregation to sing the first verse of "Silent Night" with the choir and congregation in the darkened church.)

Prayer: God, thank you for the birth of Jesus and the joy and wonder his coming among us brings. Amen.

Christmas Day
God With Us

John 1:1-14

A long time ago the king said, "Everyone go to the place where you were born, sign your name there, and pay your taxes."

When Joseph heard what the king had commanded, he said, "Bethlehem is far away. Mary is going to have a baby. What shall I do?"

Joseph walked up and down the dirt floor, thinking, "What shall I do?" Then he knew. "We will go to Bethlehem," he said, aloud.

Mary packed their things and sang, thinking of the baby that was soon to be born and become part of their family.

Joseph said to the donkey, "We are going to Bethlehem. You will carry Mary on your back."

The donkey brayed, "Hee-haw," happily, thinking of carrying Mary to Bethlehem.

Mary, Joseph, and the donkey traveled a long, long time. It was very late when they reached Bethlehem. The city was crowded with visitors.

"Do you have a place where we may stay tonight?" Joseph asked, knocking on door after door.

"Go away. No room!" was all he heard over and over and over. "Go away."

Joseph was sad. Nowhere to stay!

Mary was tired. Nowhere to sleep!

The donkey was hungry. Nothing to eat!

Then a kind innkeeper said, "There is a stable where I keep my cows and sheep. You may stay there and I will bring you some food."

Mary, Joseph, and the donkey went to the stable. It was warm and clean and quiet. Mary fell asleep. The donkey nibbled on the hay.

In the fields shepherds were watching their sheep. One of the shepherds felt the cold wind and said to the lamb in his lap, "It is going to be a cold night, little lamb."

"Baaah," agreed the little lamb.

There was no time, however, to worry over warmth, for suddenly they heard singing. A bright light filled the sky and they heard an angel sing, "Glory be to God! This night in Bethlehem a babe is born who will be the king, as God has promised. Go to Bethlehem."

The shepherds ran to Bethlehem. They went into the stable. There in the manger lay a baby boy. The shepherds prayed, "Thank you, God."

Then they asked, "What is the baby's name?"

Joseph replied, "His name is Jesus." For he was the "*Word* of God" in flesh, in body.

The shepherds said, "His name is Jesus, Emmanuel, God-with-us." Then they returned to care for their sheep.

Talk together: Who is Jesus? Where was Jesus born? Who were his parents?

Prayer: God, we thank you for your Word and your words and your care. Help us share that love this Christmas. Amen.

First Sunday After Christmas
Jesus The Learner

Luke 2:41-52

"Where is Jesus?" Mary asked Joseph. "I thought he was with his friend Samuel, but I have not seen him for some time."

"I will go look for him," Joseph replied.

The family had traveled to Jerusalem for the Passover and were returning home to Nazareth, Jesus, now twelve, was allowed to travel with his friend, Samuel, and his family.

When Joseph returned, he had not found Jesus. Mary and Joseph were worried. They asked up and down the line of pilgrims who had come to the Passover if they had seen Jesus. It was then that Samuel came to Mary and Joseph.

"Jesus said he was going to stay in Jerusalem and ..." Samuel began, but Mary and Joseph did not wait for Samuel to finish his sentence. They quickly turned to walk the road back to Jerusalem and Jesus.

For three long days they searched. The parents were in a panic. Where could he be?

As they walked into the Temple to pray for God's guidance, they saw Jesus sitting with the teachers, listening and asking questions.

"Why did the big fish swallow Jonah?"

"Why did the bush Moses saw not burn up?"

"Why did Cain hate Abel?"

"Why did Jacob cheat Esau?"

"Did the raven really feed Elijah?"

The questions went on and on because Jesus was curious. Because he was curious, he was wise, as well.

Together the family returned to Nazareth where Jesus grew in size and stature, in wisdom and experience, in favor with God and the people.

Talk together: Why did Jesus stay behind in Jerusalem? What would you have asked the teachers? What question about God would you like to ask?

Prayer: Dear God, we thank you for your blessings of knowledge and wisdom and faith imagination. Help us remember, however, that it is more important to love and trust you than to know. Amen.

Second Sunday After Christmas
God's Book

John 1:10-18

No one had ever seen God, so God, the Great Creator, decided to write a Book. "With my words I will tell the people who I am and what my plan is." (Have a Bible in your lap and show it to the children.)

But, being a reader of words, God knew that words should not tell but show, so God, the Great Author, became the *Word* in flesh and blood to live among us.

And they called his name Jesus.

Talk together: What book did God write? How did God write it?

John wrote in his Gospel, "The good news of God": "And the Word became flesh and lived among us, and we have seen his glory, the glory as of a father's only son, full of grace and truth."

As we say together John's words, which I have just read, ponder on who "The Word of God" is for you.

Prayer: Dear God, although no one has seen you because you are Spirit, we thank you for showing us your Son who makes you known. Amen.

Epiphany
The Three Magi

Matthew 2:1-12

Children enjoy drama, especially when they can gather in the front of the sanctuary to watch and hear the youth or adults act out "The Three Magi." Perhaps older children might read the script themselves.

Characters
Narrator
Three wise men (or women) — Faith, Hope, and Love each wearing a placard with his or her name

Faith: *(Excitedly)* We saw it! We did see it! Remember the night when the warm breeze blew in from the sea and that one star shone so brightly it seemed to say, "Have faith. Come, follow me."

Hope: I hope so. We have traveled so far, all I have left is hope.

Narrator: The days since the Magi left on their quest to search for the Child by following the star have lengthened into months.

Faith: I believe. I have faith that we will find the Child.

Hope: I hope so. I only hope so!

Faith: It is not hope but faith that matters.

Hope: I hope so.

Faith and Hope: Yet we would not have reached this far had it not been for your love and care. *(Turn toward Love)*

Faith: Remember the night you traveled through dark and dangerous woods to get medicine to heal our sickness?

Hope: And when we had no food, you begged among the people.

Faith: I have faith you will be rewarded.

Hope: I hope so, too!

Narrator: The third Magi smiled in appreciation.

Faith: We will soon be there. I know we will.

Hope: *(Slowly)* I hope so.

Love: But look, the star has disappeared.

Faith: No, I see a faint light ahead over the small village we are approaching.

Hope: *(With enthusiasm)* I hope so!

Narrator: As the Magi came into the village, they saw that the people were very poor. The beggars crowded around the three Magi, begging for food and money.

Faith: I have faith the star will appear again.

Hope: I ... hope ... so ...

Love: Look, the people need us here right where we are, so this is where we belong. Let us stay here and share what we have.

Narrator: The three Magi agreed. Faith lifted the children onto her camel and told them about the special star and the importance of faith to make the impossible possible. Hope sat in the center of a group of the village elders and told them the power of the persistence of hope. Love fed and healed the people.

The three Magi were so busy, showing who they were as faith, hope, and love, they did not see the star reappear, for their search for the Child had ended. He was there among them.

Talk together: Today is Epiphany Sunday. Epiphany means "showing," as Faith, Hope, and Love showed who they were by what they did. The three Wise Men showed their love by bringing gifts to the Child. Who was the Child?

Prayer: Dear God, as you showed us your love through Jesus, help us to show our love by how we live. In Christ's name we pray. Amen.

Reading The Christmas Eve Scriptures

Stan Purdum

Introduction

Scripture has immense power in its own right, but when presented aloud in public, its impact on hearers can be increased or diminished depending upon presentation. We've all heard passages read so poorly in worship that the content of verses is barely communicated. Likewise we've heard scripture read clearly, but with such lack of expression that the impact is lost on the audience.

When read both clearly and with feeling, however, scripture can open hearers to the living word of God.

The selection included here is nothing other than scripture, hand-picked verses from Matthew, Luke, and John, all lines that most church attendees will have heard many times. But they have been organized so that themes introduced in one set of verses are picked up in the next, linking the events of Christmas with those of Holy Week and Easter.

This interlaced reading can be presented effectively by two readers who have taken the time to read and understand the material beforehand, and are able to read it out loud with the appropriate inflection and emotional tone. (I have supplied the scripture references for your convenience, but do not have the speakers say them.)

But for maximum impact, I suggest that well ahead of time, you give the reading to two people who have dramatic ability (and preferably contrasting voices), and ask them to memorize the lines. Then during your service, have the two performers stand in opposite corners of the chancel, with Voice 1 speaking his or her lines and then Voice 2 coming in with the other lines as soon as the first speaker finishes. Encourage the performers to use their hands dramatically as they would in animated conversation. If your sanctuary has spotlights, you can enhance the presentation by darkening the room and then spotlighting each performer in turn as he or she speaks.

In my church, my daughter and I served as the two voices and each spoke from memory, "feeling" the words as we spoke. The effect was powerful.

The Interlaced Scripture Reading

Voice 1: In those days a decree went out from Emperor Augustus that all the world should be registered. This was the first registration and was taken while Quirinius was governor of Syria. All went to their own towns to be registered. Joseph also went from the town of Nazareth in Galilee to Judea, to the city of David called Bethlehem, because he was descended from the house and family of Dávid. He went to be registered with Mary, to whom he was engaged and who was expecting a child. (Luke 2:1-5)

Voice 2: While they were there, the time came for her to deliver her child. And she gave birth to her firstborn son and wrapped him in bands of cloth, and laid him in a manger, because there was no place for them in the inn. (Luke 2:6-7)

Voice 1: Now there was a good and righteous man named Joseph, who ... was waiting expectantly for the kingdom of God. This man went to Pilate and asked for the body of Jesus. Then he took it down, wrapped it in a linen cloth, and laid it in a rock-hewn tomb where no one had ever been laid. (Luke 23:50-53)

Voice 2: In that region there were shepherds living in the fields, keeping watch over their flock by night. Then an angel of the Lord stood before them, and the glory of the Lord shone around them, and they were terrified. (Luke 2:8-9)

Voice 1: After the sabbath, as the first day of the week was dawning, Mary Magdalene and the other Mary went to see the tomb. And suddenly there was a great earthquake; for an angel of the Lord, descending from heaven, came and rolled back the stone and sat on it. His appearance was like lightning, and his clothing white as snow. For fear of him the guards shook and became like dead men. (Matthew 28:1-4)

Voice 2: But the angel said to them, "Do not be afraid; for see — I am bringing you good news of great joy for all the people: to you is born this day in the city of David a Savior, who is the Messiah, the Lord." (Luke 2:10-11)

Voice 1: But the angel said to the women, "Do not be afraid; I know that you are looking for Jesus who was crucified. He is not here; for he has been raised, as he said." (Matthew 28:5-6)

Voice 2: "This will be a sign for you: you will find a child wrapped in bands of cloth and lying in a manger." And suddenly there was with the angel a multitude of the heavenly host, praising God and saying, "Glory to God in the highest heaven, and on earth peace among those whom he favors!" (Luke 2:12-14)

Voice 1: [And Jesus said to them,] Peace I leave with you; my peace I give to you ... Do not let your hearts be troubled, and do not let them be afraid. (John 14:27)

Voice 2: When the angels had left them and gone into heaven, the shepherds said to one another, "Let us go now to Bethlehem and see this thing that has taken place, which the Lord has made known to us." So they went with haste and found Mary and Joseph, and the child lying in a manger. (Luke 2:15-16)

Voice 1: A week later his disciples were again in the house, and Thomas was with them. Although the doors were shut, Jesus came and stood among them and said, "Peace be with you." Then he said to Thomas, "Put your finger here and see my hands. Reach out your hand and put it in my side. Do not doubt but believe." Thomas answered him, "My Lord and my God!" (John 20:26-28)

Voice 2: When they saw this, they made known what had been told them about this child; and all who heard it were amazed at what the shepherds told them. But Mary treasured all these words and pondered them in her heart. The shepherds returned, glorifying and praising God for all they had heard and seen, as it had been told them. (Luke 2:17-20)

Voice 1: Now Jesus did many other signs in the presence of his disciples, which are not written in this book. (John 20:30)

Voice 2: But these are written so that you may come to believe that Jesus is the Messiah, the Son of God, and that through believing you may have life in his name. (John 20:31)

Contributors

Elaine M. Ward is a storyteller/writer/preacher who served for nearly twenty years as Minister of Children at University Park United Methodist Church in Dallas, Texas. She is a graduate of Capital University, Union Theological Seminary (New York City), and Lancaster Theological Seminary, where she was writer-in-residence for seven years. Now a resident of Austin, Texas, Ward is the author of *Asking For Wonder, And The Sea Lay Down, Alleluia!* and *Story Time At The Altar* (CSS), as well as *Love In A Lunchbox: Poems And Parables For Children's Worship* (Abingdon).

R. H. Thompson is a former elementary school teacher who is now a freelance writer and teacher as well as a full-time mom in Calgary, Alberta, Canada. She is a graduate of Edge Hill University College, Lancashire, England (B.Ed.).

David H. Covington is an associate professor of English at North Carolina State University specializing in professional writing and Victorian literature. An active member of the Kirk of Kildare (Presbyterian) in Cary, North Carolina, he is a graduate of the University of Florida (B.A.) and Vanderbilt University (M.A., Ph.D.).

Janet K. Gardner earned her B.A. degree in Communication Arts from California Lutheran University, where she also worked for six years as the Supervisor of Events Services. She enjoys teaching Sunday school and is the author of *Bible Bingo* (CSS). Gardner is a resident of Thousand Oaks, California.

Rochelle M. Pennington is a writer and consultant who has worked with several well-known authors, including Jack Canfield (*Chicken Soup for the Soul*), H. Jackson Brown (*Life's Little Instruction Book*), and Alice Gray (*Stories for the Heart*). Pennington is the co-author (with H. Jackson Brown) of *Highlighted in Yellow*, and her writing has been included in multiple *Chicken Soup for the Soul* and *Stories for the Heart* volumes. She is also a contributing author to *Ripples of Joy* and *Living Life on Purpose*. She writes *Insights and Inspirations*, a syndicated weekly newspaper column appearing in several Wisconsin newspapers. Pennington and her family live in Campbellsport, Wisconsin.

Mary Connealy has a bachelor's degree in mass media from Wayne State College, Wayne, Nebraska. She serves her church as a Sunday school teacher, superintendent, and newsletter editor, and has a busy life as a full-time wife and mother who assists her husband on their dairy farm in Decatur, Nebraska.

Cynthia E. Cowen is a prolific and enthusiastic writer who has produced many worship resources for CSS Publishing Company. She serves as an Associate in Ministry in Youth and Family at Our Saviour's Lutheran Church in Iron Mountain, Michigan, and also serves on several synod and denominational leadership teams, including six years on the Executive Board of the Women of the ELCA. Cowen holds a B.A. degree in education from Northern Michigan University, is a graduate of the Northern Great Lakes Synod Lay School for Mission, and is a licensed lay minister at Calvary Lutheran Church, Quinnasec, Michigan. She has been certified in youth ministry at Wartburg Seminary.

Stan Purdum is the pastor of Centenary United Methodist Church in Waynesburg, Ohio. He is also the editor of the preaching journal *Emphasis*, and has written extensively for both the religious and secular press. Purdum is the author of *Roll Around Heaven All Day* and *Playing In Traffic*, both accounts of his long-distance bicycle journeys, as well as *New Mercies I See* (CSS), a collection of parish stories revealing God's grace.